KEYS TO INVESTING IN GOVERNMENT SECURITIES

Second Edition

KEYS TO INVESTING IN GOVERNMENT SECURITIES

Second Edition

Jay Goldinger

Investment Counselor, Capital Insight
Beverly Hills, California

All inquiries should be addressed to:
Barron's Educational Series, Inc.
250 Wireless Boulevard
Hauppauge, NY 11788

Library of Congress Catalog Card Number 94-4015-0

International Standard Book Number 0-8120-9150-7

Library of Congress Cataloging-in-Publication Data
Goldinger, Jay.
　　Keys to investing in government securities / Jay Goldinger.—
　　2nd ed.
　　　　p.　cm.
　　Includes index.
　　ISBN 0-8120-9150-7
　　1. Government securities—United States. I. Title.
　　HG4936.G65　　1995
　　332.63'232—dc20

　　　　　　　　　　　　　　　　　　94-40150
　　　　　　　　　　　　　　　　　　CIP

PRINTED IN THE UNITED STATES OF AMERICA

5678　5500　987654321

CONTENTS

Introduction **vii**

1. A Tour of the Federal Reserve **1**
2. Bank Reserves: How the Fed Moves the Market **5**
3. Primary Dealers: Uncle Sam's Biggest and Best Customers **8**
4. Treasury Bills: Better than Cash for the Conservative Investor **11**
5. Purchasing Treasury Bills **14**
6. Treasury Notes: More Risk, More Reward, Still Safe **19**
7. T-Notes for Income Investing **22**
8. The Safety of a Treasury Instrument **25**
9. The Most Volatile Treasuries **28**
10. Zero-coupon Governments: The Pros and Cons of "STRIPS" **32**
11. Stripped Treasuries: Shopping Hard Before You Buy **34**
12. How the Yield Curve Can Set You Straight **37**
13. How to Find a Bond Broker **42**
14. How to Read the Financial Pages **45**
15. Building a Consensus View of the Market **49**
16. Government Agency Bonds: More Yield, Less Liquidity **53**
17. Treasury Futures: Upping the Ante on Risk and Reward **57**
18. Limiting Risk with Futures **61**
19. Options on Treasury Futures: Welcome to the Casino **65**
20. The View from Abroad **68**

21. Monitoring Global Markets Can Help Investors at Home **71**
22. Taxes and Treasuries: It's Net, not Yield, that Counts **74**
23. Municipal Bonds: Tax-free but not Risk-free **78**
24. The Art of Investing in Munis **83**
25. Savings Bonds: A Safe and Shrewd Investment **87**
26. Savings Bonds: A Tax-wise Way to Pay for College **90**
27. Mutual Funds: Where Wall Street Crosses Main Street **93**
28. The Fundamentals of Government Bond Fund Investing **97**
29. Your Bond Fund Goal: Capital Preservation **99**
30. Choosing a Government Bond Fund: Ask the Hard Questions **102**
31. Financial Derivatives Can Bedevil Fund Investors **106**
32. Watching Fund Expenses **110**
33. Bond Funds: Finding the Best Deal **113**
34. Bond Funds: Free Canapés and Costly Lunches **116**
35. Keeping an Open Mind About Closed-end Funds **119**
36. The Downside of Muni Bond Funds **121**
37. Hard Truths and Smart Strategies for Informed Investors **124**

Questions and Answers **127**
Glossary **134**
Appendix **141**
Index **159**

INTRODUCTION

During a twenty-year career as a bond broker investing my clients' money and my own in the U.S. Government securities markets here and around the world, I've learned the hard way how to win and lose. Currently, as chief investment strategist at Capital Insight Brokerage and, previously, as a member of the team with Cantor, Fitzgerald & Company, I've watched how Wall Street sells the concept of treasuries to Main Street.

It doesn't.

For the most part, *institutional investors*—banks, pensions and other retirement funds, mutual funds and other investment firms—dominate the U.S. Treasury markets. They know, from a credit-risk standpoint, that treasuries are the safest investment in the world; they have no default worries. From a market-risk standpoint, such investors have access to the best information and the finest money management minds to limit their losses and produce profits—in sick or in healthy economic times.

What about Main Street? Most individual investors generally stick with treasury bills, short-term and safe, and rarely venture beyond. No surprise here. The U.S. Government bond market, despite its size, strength, and safety record, is about as familiar to investors as the far side of the moon. The fact is that stockbrokers feel comfortable selling stocks and packaged investments with more action and bigger commissions. Bond brokers are a rare breed; the best ones who have mastered the market are investing their own money and work with a limited number of knowledgeable clients. They don't peddle, cold call, or dial for dollars.

And that's exactly why I wrote this book. I wanted to make you, the reader, street savvy while giving you a guided tour of what is probably the most fascinating of all investments once you understand how the U.S. Government bond market really works. I wanted to arm you with the information you need to make a profit on treasuries regardless of the economic climate.

We'll start with the basics, and you'll see that the bond market is very different from the stock market. The bond market is almost totally driven by changes in interest rates. Remember this fundamental truth: Interest rates go up but treasury bill, note, and bond prices go down. Interest rates go down but prices go up. No earnings per share to watch, industry health to worry about, or consumer buying habits to track. Those are fundamentals of the stock market, not the bond market.

With treasuries, you must keep plugged in on a more macroeconomic scale, and I'll show you how to do that. Monitoring the economic statistics that are issued regularly out of Washington D.C. helps you gauge inflationary pressures. Watching the Federal Reserve and anticipating what it is about to do helps you keep in perspective how the rest of the world thinks those policymakers will be acting. This is one case where it pays, literally, to be an informed investor.

And it's much easier to be informed today than five years ago when I wrote the first edition. Today, with CNN, CNBC, and the popularity of on-line databasing, it is no longer the case of one investor having more or better information than another. Now, investment decision-makers have instantaneous access to a torrent of worldwide information. With this global access to opinions and events-in-the-making, now, more than ever, markets move on expectations, instead of reacting to news.

However, before this information can be really useful to your portfolio, you must determine for yourself what type of investor and risk-taker you are. Fundamentally, there are three kinds.

Are you a short-term trader trying to hit singles, moving in and out of the market with lightning speed, limiting your risk, but always in the game, ready to go to bat? If so, you need to be vigilant; this is a 24-hour, five-day-a-week, extremely competitive market. What is important to a trader is not what's happening today but what you believe will happen tomorrow. Here's a perfect example: just before the Iraq-Kuwait war, U.S. Secretary of State James Baker was trying to hammer out a settlement. When he came out of the negotiating room to face the crowd of reporters, I saw the gloomy look on his face and sold treasury bonds. I had a hunch no agreement had been reached and the Middle Eastern war would start. I was lucky; I was right, and I bought back the bonds within minutes, turning a quick profit. But this is trading and not a suitable investment strategy for 99 percent of the investing public. Remember, a bond trader's outlook is measured in minutes; long term is an hour.

Are you an intermediate-term investor? Do you feel comfortable with investments that have a buy/hold/sell horizon of a few months to one or two years? If so, you will be influenced by changes in reality, not changes in expectations. For example, after years of easing the U.S. monetary policy, the Federal Reserve Board changed course dramatically in February 1994. It abruptly tightened monetary policy by raising short-term interest rates—i.e., the Federal Funds rate and the bank discount rate. The intermediate-term investor recognizes the Fed is a large cruise ship, not a swift turn-on-a-dime speedboat, and took this as a sign that interest rates would be headed higher for the next six to eighteen months. The wise intermediate investor would have pruned his or her portfolio and replaced long-term bonds with short (under two year) maturities.

You may be a long-term investor. Your time horizon is usually two to ten years and depends on extreme shifts in the marketplace. You will try to time the market—buy on the lows and sell on the highs—but you will never be precise and may miss the bottom or the top by months. The long-term investor is driven either by incredible value or a rich, possibly inflated price. For example, in the early 1980s, interest rates on medium-term notes were driven to 15 percent. This offered tremendous value to the long-term investors who slowly accumulated these notes and were rewarded with historic yields, while waiting for interest rates to decline. Their patience paid off. By the early 1990s, short-term interest rates had dropped to levels of between 3 to 4 percent. New bond investors had very little chance for appreciation as the long-term value investors took their profits and sold out.

Many lessons were learned over the last decade and a half. Amazingly, in the early 1980s, investors shunned high-yielding medium-term bonds when they should have been scooping them up by the carload. Yet, in the early 1990s, they were loading up on two-year treasury notes paying 4 percent. Ironic. These T-note investors would have needed interest rates to go below zero in order to earn the same price appreciation that was literally dumped in their laps several years before.

The fallacy here is that investors are constantly motivated by past performance. That may be okay in the stock market, where stocks can double and triple in price on a variety of factors—earnings, contracts, a new product, intense Wall Street support. But interest rates drive bonds, and playing this game is very similar to trading a stock that can only go between zero and $20. Would you buy a stock at $19 when your maximum profit could only be $1? Of course not, but that's just what a majority of investors did in the early 1990s when they stampeded into bonds and bond funds. Investors were buying bond funds in January 1994, based on the performance of the fund two years earlier—yet those strong portfolio gains were achieved in a period of declining interest rates. With rates climbing in 1994, that performance could not possibly be duplicated.

Now here is where it pays to stay aware and informed. Do not use the same criteria for selecting a stock fund to choose a bond fund. And do not expect the bond fund manager to do your homework for you. Certainly it is not in the fund's best interest for the manager to tell you, with a straight face, "Rates are moving up; it is time to get out of the fund." Not when he makes his living by your staying in.

The same is true for buyers of individual bonds. Be informed and find a broker who will serve your interests, not just his or her own commission motivations. For instance, if you want to buy treasuries on leverage, make sure you get the "repo" rate, not the broker loan rate for margining stocks that could be one to two points higher. The repo rate is lower because there is no credit risk on treasuries as there is on stocks. Also, ask your broker how much the markup is on your purchase. That's the spread between the bid and the ask price, and it's definitely wider for individual investors buying smaller blocks of bonds than it is for institutional investors.

Information. It's as crucial today as knowing your investment goals, comfort zones, and the type of investor you are—trader, intermediate-term, or medium-term. But whether you invest through mutual funds or with a seasoned broker (and be sure to find one who is a winner when investing his or her own money), you cannot exist in an informational vacuum. You need an edge.

I've written this book for one reason: to give you that edge.

Jay Goldinger
November 1, 1994

1

A TOUR OF THE FEDERAL RESERVE

The second most powerful and influential person in the United States after the president is not the vice-president, not the chief justice of the Supreme Court, and not the chairman of the New York Stock Exchange. It is the chairman of the Board of Governors of the Federal Reserve Board. Apart from the presidential pronouncements on tax policy, the Fed chairman's decisions have the single greatest impact on the economy—at home and abroad and on investors in U.S. Government securities.

The chairman of the Federal Reserve controls the twin faucets of cash and credit that feed the U.S. monetary system. In truth, he largely controls short-term interest rates, capital borrowing, and corporate and economic growth.

The Fed chairman, although appointed by the president for a four-year term, answers to no one. He does deliver a report to the Congress twice a year as mandated by the Humphrey-Hawkins Full-Growth Employment Investment Act and makes other periodic appearances. In theory, though, he is—and should be—free of political pressure, although that is not always the case. The White House and Congress often make their feelings known, subtly, of course. Indeed, almost halfway through the 1990s, the Fed seems to be a bit more political than in the past. During the 1993 State of the Union address, Fed Chairman Alan Greenspan was sitting next to First Lady Hillary Clinton while her husband delivered his report. Nevertheless, as the architect of U.S. monetary policy, the Fed chairman has the delicate yet demanding task of regulating the flow of credit to promote orderly, sustained economic expansion without triggering inflation.

1

Now what does this mean in plain English? Simply that you should understand how the Fed works and keep an eye on what it does. As an investor, it affects your bottom line.

Established by Congress in 1913 as a central bank for the United States so commercial banks could meet demands by farmers for cash and currency to plant and harvest crops, the Fed today is a network of twelve Federal Reserve Banks, plus branches.

The heart and soul of the Federal Reserve is the Federal Open Market Committee (FOMC). Membership is comprised of the seven-person Federal Reserve Board of Governors plus the presidents of the twelve Federal Reserve Banks. The FOMC, which meets eight times a year to set and fine-tune monetary policy, has two goals: first, curb inflation by maintaining the extremely delicate balance between cash, credit, and debt and, second, promote a healthy long-term economic environment by preserving the value of the dollar.

How does the Fed adjust monetary policy to achieve these twin goals? Mainly by controlling the cash and credit faucets through buying or selling U.S. Government securities. This, in turn, builds or reduces bank reserves as the economy expands or contracts. It also sets targets for bank reserves, percentage parameters for money supply growth, a desired range for Fed funds interest rates, and a total figure for non-financial debt.

As Joseph Coyne, chief spokesperson for the Federal Reserve, puts it in summing up the Fed's broad objectives, "Keeping inflation under control is crucial for sustained long-term economic growth. Over the years, we've learned that inflation causes recessions, and too much money causes inflation."

Think of the Fed's Federal Open Market Committee as the economy's accelerator or its brake pedal. For example, when members of the FOMC think the economy is slowing down, they can press down on the accelerator—pump cash into circulation—by going into the marketplace and buying treasury bills, notes, or bonds.

If the FOMC feels the economy is overheating and inflation will make existing dollars worth less, it will put on the brakes by selling treasury securities it owns, thus removing money from circulation.

Whose foot is actually on the gas and brake pedals? It is a battery of people who work on what is called the Open Market Desk. If the Federal Open Market Committee is indeed the heart and soul of the Federal Reserve, the Open Market Desk is the nerve center. Tucked away on the eighth floor of the Federal Reserve Bank of New York, the Desk carries out, on a daily basis, the FOMC's monetary policy directives.

Every day at precisely 11:40 A.M. Eastern Time, Fedwatchers around the world, economists and professional investors, have their eyes and ears trained on the Open Market Desk. That's when the Fed's daily operations are executed, adding or draining cash—actually bank reserves—to (or from) the economy to keep the country's monetary policy on track for the next 24 hours. Unlike Congress, which has galleries where people can watch the action, the Open Market Desk conducts its operations in virtual secrecy. Many Fed employees themselves have never been in the busy room on the eighth floor.

The Fed, however, has been quietly undergoing some changes, and you don't have to be a professional Fedwatcher to spot them. In 1994, the Fed started acting like a sound-money central bank similar to one that you would find in Germany, Japan, England, or Switzerland. Historically, these banks and others in trade-dependent nations act and anticipate rather than react. In 1994, the Fed quelled inflationary fears and stabilized the markets, telegraphing its decisions. How? By releasing a press statement on the day the FOMC met, briefly explaining its actions and what the impact on investors was likely to be. One precedent-setting announcement occurred on February 4, 1994, when the Fed said, "The FOMC decided to increase slightly the degree of pressure on reserve positions. The action is expected to be associated with a small increase in short-term money market interest rates."

A spokesperson for the Fed said no formal policy has been introduced to publicize FOMC actions on a regular basis. In fact, minutes of FOMC meetings are still released six weeks later, a curious and seemingly antiquated practice in a day when there is a growing sophistication—and hunger—among investors for government information that moves markets. However, change comes slowly at the Federal Reserve Board, and still another change is the Fed's recent concern about the health of the U.S. dollar. Now it is a top priority of the Fed along with regulating the money supply, minimizing inflation, and helping to keep the business engine humming, productive, and fully employed. The Fed, through its new activeness and openness, is slowly building credibility for itself with foreign investors worldwide, while implementing monetary policy change without rocking markets. It all adds up to a new sense of stability in the markets and that's good news for investors in U.S. Government securities.

2

BANK RESERVES: HOW THE FED MOVES THE MARKET

What makes the Open Market Desk the single most powerful financial decision-making venue in the world? The answer goes back to the roots of the commercial banking system.

By federal law, banks and all depository institutions—mutual savings banks, savings and loans, credit unions—must meet minimum reserve requirements. For every checking account deposit on its books, a bank must set aside 10 percent of the dollar amount as a reserve. This can be stored as either cash in its own vault or cash placed in a non-interest bearing account at one of the twelve regional Federal Reserve Banks.

Think of these bank reserve accounts as being the bank's own checking account, with the Fed managing them and having sole depository and check-writing privileges. These reserve accounts transact the internal functions of check cashing. For example, when your bank accepts your check drawn on another bank, the check is cleared by electronically crediting your bank's reserve account and debiting the reserve account at the bank on which your check was drawn.

Historically, the Fed's reserve requirements have been thought of primarily as the best way to maintain a bank's liquidity so that the institution would have the cash to meet a customer's withdrawal or to cover any losses of funds. Recently, however, the Federal Deposit Insurance Corporation and the Fed's role as the lender of last resort have removed the liquidity burdens from bank reserves. Today, bank reserves are generally considered to be a monetary policy tool that can be adjusted and fine-tuned by the Open Market Desk.

Here's how that is accomplished. When the Fed wants to adjust monetary policy, it either buys or sells U.S. Government securities. To ease credit and promote economic growth, the Fed buys very short-term securities in the open market from one of its primary dealers. It pays for the securities by electronically crediting the bank with funds on deposit, which are the equivalent of cash. With this new influx of money, the bank must set aside approximately 10 percent of it as reserves. The deposit, minus the reserves, gives the bank more money to lend out. Hence, the Fed has pumped more money into the system, credit is eased, and theoretically, economic expansion is promoted.

Now, to tighten credit and slow economic growth, the Fed does the reverse. It sells U.S. Government securities from its own inventory to a primary dealer and takes the money it receives out of circulation and out of the monetary system. At the same time, when the primary dealer pays for the securities it has just bought from the Fed, the bank reserves set aside for the dealer's money are eliminated. The process is called "draining the reserves." And with reduced deposits and fewer reserves, the bank has less money to lend. With fewer funds to lend, the bank would put its money out at a higher interest rate; some borrowers will resist and economic growth is discouraged. Thus the Fed has achieved its goal of reducing the money supply and tightening credit, a tactic used to combat inflation. It also controls the currency or cash in circulation. (See Key 1 on money supply.)

Suppose that banks need additional reserves to meet higher loan demand. They are not supposed to rely on the Fed to shore up these reserves when they run short. They can bypass the Fed and borrow money overnight, or for longer periods, from other banks with excess reserves. This is called the Federal Funds market, and the rate of interest, called the Federal Funds Rate, is set by the institutions but influenced by the Fed. The Fed Funds Rate is a critical credit barometer because almost all short-term rates—and yields—react to a change in the Fed Funds Rate.

On the other hand, long-term interest rates are primarily determined by inflationary expectations.

The Open Market Desk manager has a variety of tools at his disposal to influence monetary policy on a day-to-day basis. As an alternative to permanent sales or purchases of U.S. Government securities, to add to or drain bank reserves, a more common strategy is to use a repurchase agreement, sometimes known as an "RP" or a "repo." This is a temporary purchase of government securities, usually for one day but it can be for as long as seven days.

For instance, if the Fed wants to create reserves, the Desk purchases government securities in the open market from a primary dealer or foreign central bank and agrees to sell them back to the institution the following day at the same rate plus interest.

The opposing strategy is a "matched sale," or what is sometimes called a "reverse repo." This is a tool used by the Fed to drain reserves and tighten the money supply. To execute a matched sale, the Open Market Desk sells U.S. Government securities to a primary dealer or a foreign central bank, agreeing to buy them back on a specific date, usually in one to seven days, at the same price.

The question you are probably asking yourself is this: "As a private investor, do I really have to be a daily Fedwatcher to be successful?" Absolutely not. But you should pay attention to FOMC actions, as they are reported in the press, and keep on top of the monthly and quarterly announcements and pronouncements that come out of Washington, D.C.

Information, as much as you can get, gives you—above all—the edge you need to invest intelligently in U.S. Government securities. One of the best sources for information on the Federal Reserve is from the Fed itself. Each of the twelve Federal Reserve Banks issues reports, at least quarterly, that are available to the public. Contact the public affairs office of the Bank nearest you.

3

PRIMARY DEALERS: UNCLE SAM'S BIGGEST AND BEST CUSTOMERS

When the U.S. Treasury needs money to run the country, it holds auctions and sells bills, notes, and bonds to the highest bidder. Private investors, of course, can buy directly from the Treasury. But the U.S. Government's biggest customers, who buy an average of 80 to 90 percent of new federal debt at Treasury auctions, are called primary dealers.

Primary dealers are also called "market makers"—they maintain an inventory of treasury issues and can sell them into the market to break a logjam; that is, when everyone is a buyer and prices are rising.

On the flip side of that coin, primary dealers have the financial muscle with which to buy the excess treasuries when investors are selling. But they are not required to step in and stabilize the market; they must only quote a bid or an ask, and it doesn't have to be the lowest or highest. In short, primary dealers help the Federal Reserve—the nation's central bank—regulate the money supply.

Who are these primary dealers? They are 39 financial institutions worldwide—familiar names like Merrill Lynch, Lehman Brothers, Goldman Sachs, Citicorp, Bear Stearns—plus international banks and brokerages such as Fuji Bank, Nikko Securities, Nomura Securities, Daiwa, UBS (United Bank of Switzerland), among others.

The primary dealer's role has changed dramatically in the past four years. "Primary dealers are now trading for their own account rather than strictly being a market

8

maker," says Joe Rogers, senior vice-president in charge of dealer trading for Greenwich Capital Markets of Greenwich, Connecticut. Why? Technology plus a surge of capital into the government securities market has narrowed the spread between the bid and offer—the difference being the primary dealers' compensation for keeping a market in balance.

New technology lets investors instantaneously sleuth out the most favorable bid/offer prices, and newcomers are settling for a thinner profit.

Primary dealers no longer have the herculean financial brawn to influence markets, notes Rogers. The "more aggressive" hedge funds—investment partnerships that take huge risks in order to score a whopping profit—are attracting more capital and more experienced traders, he says, and this has drained some of the liquidity out of Wall Street.

To earn the primary dealer designation and, thus, the opportunity to bid on huge lots of treasuries at auction, the Federal Reserve Board says it must have "enough confidence" in the financial institution to deal with it as a major customer. Previously, the Fed required a primary dealer to have the financial muscle to buy or finance enough treasuries to account for 1 percent of the total secondary, or resale, market. But since that number always fluctuated so sharply, the benchmark was dropped.

The Fed does say that today some $170 billion in U.S. Treasury securities, on average, trade daily in the secondary market, up from $100 billion four years ago. However, the total public debt comprised of outstanding treasury bills, notes, and bonds and some federal financing securities stood at $3.1 trillion as of August 31, 1994. Unfortunately, it is growing by the second. Four years ago, the public debt was $2 trillion.

Remember, the 39 primary dealers and other financial institutions that aspire to this designation do not simply warehouse treasuries as a favor to the U.S. Government. They are continually buying and selling bills, notes, and bonds, usually to and from each other, trying to earn a profit on every trade.

They also wholesale huge blocks of government bonds to pension funds, mutual funds, banks, and other institutions, and they fill the buy/sell orders of individual investors that are placed through the nation's 5,350 brokerage firms.

However, as an individual investor buying the U.S. Government securities individually, rather than through a mutual fund, you should hope your personal broker does not have a cozy relationship with just one primary dealer. The U.S. Government bond market is a global bazaar with at least 39 mercenary merchants all scrambling for the best profit. Just make sure someone is haggling hard on your behalf.

4

TREASURY BILLS: BETTER THAN CASH FOR THE CONSERVATIVE INVESTOR

The first treasury bill was sold in 1929—the year, coincidentally, the stock market suffered its first major crash.

That T-bill, however, was redeemed at maturity, on schedule, and in the more than six decades since then, Uncle Sam has always paid off his IOUs.

That's exactly what a treasury bill is. The federal government borrows money weekly to keep its cash flowing—to meet its expenses while waiting to collect its income. And of all the IOUs issued, T-bills, backed by the full faith and credit of the U.S. Treasury, are the closest certificates there are to cash.

In fact, treasury bills are liquid cash equivalents that earn income, and some think that makes them better than cash. They can be cashed out immediately, sometimes for more than 100 cents on the dollar (and sometimes for less). They are also remarkably flexible investments yielding a high, market interest rate that can be purchased at a discount. There is no commission if you buy them directly from the government. Nor are there any custodial fees.

Treasury bills (as well as treasury notes and treasury bonds discussed in following keys) are among the few remaining investments offering substantial tax advantages. Unlike other fixed-income securities—certificates of deposit (CDs), corporate bonds, or commercial paper, for example—you pay no state or local taxes on the income earned on T-bills (or coupon income on treasury notes or bonds).

Indeed, treasury bills are probably the wisest choice for investors who want absolutely no risk whatsoever and who can commit their cash for periods ranging from one week to one year. T-bills are also a smart place to park cash between investments. For instance, if you sell stocks or cash out of a retirement plan and you're looking for a cabin on the lake or a condo at the shore, T-bills are a smart place to put the proceeds, especially if interest rates are drifting downward. With T-bills, you get a yield floor—a minimum guaranteed yield or return—for at least three months, and up to a year, when held to maturity, while rates for a money market mutual fund can fluctuate daily.

On the other hand, if short-term interest rates are rising slowly, you can roll over T-bills rather than bank certificates of deposit as a conservative strategy and not worry about the price volatility that afflicts treasury notes and bonds with longer maturities.

But the hard fact is that too many investors ignore the benefits of T-bills and opt instead for certificates of deposit. This can be a big mistake. Here's why.

Investors and savers gravitate toward CDs at banks and savings and loans because they are federally insured. While this is true, they are insured only up to $100,000. And with the thrift industry and a small but startling number of banks scratching for profits, you have to wonder why one would choose a CD over a T-bill, which is also federally guaranteed and for a lot more than $100,000. In fact, there is no ceiling.

Aside from safety, certificates of deposit are not liquid, whereas treasury bills are. You can liquidate them at any time in the secondary market (see Key 5) without penalty. If you break a CD before maturity, there is generally a substantial withdrawal penalty that could cost you a hefty chunk of your interest.

The point is, as an investor, you never know when a great investment opportunity will present itself. People locked into a bank CD cannot get their money out easily to take advantage of a sound investment. With a T-bill, regardless of whether it was bought at a bank or brokerage, liquidity is a phone call away.

The key for conservative investors and savers to investing wisely in treasury bills is watching the yield spreads between T-bills and CDs. In the mid-nineties, the one-year T-bill was yielding up to 1.50 percent more than a one-year bank CD. When you factor in the tax benefits, instant liquidity, and federal guarantee that you will be paid at maturity, treasury bills are unquestionably the logical choice.

5

PURCHASING TREASURY BILLS

How are T-bills issued, bought, and sold? Basically, they come in three maturities: 13 weeks (or 91 days), 26 weeks (or 182 days), and 52 weeks (or 364 days). The minimum purchase is $10,000; $5,000 increments may be bought after that. Investors who purchase T-bills are lending the Treasury at least $10,000 for three months, six months, or a year, and that money is repaid with interest. Three- and six-month T-bills are auctioned weekly, usually on Monday (one-year T-bills are auctioned monthly on a Thursday), and the interest rate is set by market rates at that time and announced (but not set) by the Treasury.

A T-bill auction conjures up images of shouting out the price you'll pay as you would for a rare work of art or a prized Chateau Lafite Rothschild. It really isn't that adventurous. You can buy the T-bills directly from the government with no commission, or through a bank or brokerage firm that might charge you an administrative fee ranging from $25 to $60, depending on whether it is buying the bills at auction or in the secondary market. (Again, the secondary market is where previously issued T-bills are bought and sold daily.) If you hold the bills to maturity, you pay no selling commission.

However, if you sell the bills through a brokerage firm before they mature, you'll pay another $25 to $60 fee or commission. The bottom line: buy direct from the government, and save. The costliest approach is to use a treasury bill money market fund where the management fees can add unnecessary expenses that could chew up to a half percent off your investment.

Still, you can buy any treasury security (bills, notes, or bonds) directly from the Federal Reserve under a program called TREASURY DIRECT. It's a relatively simple process, and again, you pay no fees or commissions. First, you must open a TREASURY DIRECT account—you'll need to request a TREASURY DIRECT New Account Request form, PD 5182. You can obtain this form by calling or writing the Bureau of Public Debt, Department N, Washington, D.C. 20239-1500 (telephone: 202-874-4000 and have patience with the voice mail message). Or you can get one from any branch or main office of a Federal Reserve Bank. You'll be issued a TREASURY DIRECT account number when you complete and return the form.

You can also open an account automatically when you make your first TREASURY DIRECT purchase by submitting a tender. For T-bills, there are different tenders—PD 5176 for different maturities: pink for 13 weeks, yellow for 26 weeks, blue for 52 weeks. The tenders ask you to designate a bid-type: noncompetitive or competitive. Most investors will indicate noncompetitive. This means that when you put in your bid, the price you pay will be the average price of all T-bills sold that day at auction.

(The competitive bid, usually made by financial institutions buying over $1 million worth of T-bills, is a stated yield the buyer is willing to accept. But most individual investors aren't big enough buyers to be take-it-or-leave-it bidders).

To actually purchase the treasury bills, you can go to one of the thirty-six Federal Reserve Bank branch or main offices and submit the tender along with full payment for the bills up until auction time, which is 12 noon, Eastern Time. (It's best not to wait until the last minute.) The payment can either be a cashier's check, a certified personal check, cash, or other maturing treasury securities, although that may vary with different Federal Reserve Banks.

If you choose to purchase your treasury bills through the mail, the Fed must receive your payment by 10 A.M.

the morning of the auction. Again, you can mail payments and the tender direct to a Federal Reserve Bank main or branch office, or send it straight to the Bureau of Public Debt in Washington, D.C.

The rate you'll get on that auction will be quoted in the financial sections of newspapers the following day and expressed on a discount basis and possibly a coupon equivalent. For example, if 13-week T-bills were auctioned at 4.62 percent, the coupon equivalent or yield to maturity might be 4.74 percent. Because the price, also, is discounted, the $10,000 in T-bills would cost you $9,880.65.

You can sell T-bills before they mature in the highly liquid secondary market, but you will need a broker to execute the transaction. In fact, most people don't realize that they do not have to wait until the auction to buy T-bills; an experienced broker can buy—or sell—a T-bill for you 24 hours a day, Monday through Friday (markets do not trade on weekends). However, depending on market conditions, you may find that you will lose some principal if you sell before maturity. Supply and demand sets the T-bill price in the secondary market, so check out the proceeds you'll collect before you cash out.

Treasury bills can go to work for you in other ways while they are maturing. Many commercial banks and brokerages will accept T-bills as collateral if you will allow them to mature and the financial institution knows it can get its hands on cash if it has to offset your loan. In fact, bankers making secured personal loans prefer T-bills over stocks as a collateral pledge because stocks generally are more volatile and banks must monitor them closely during the life of your loan. Brokerages will also take T-bills as collateral when you purchase bonds or equities on margin.

T-bill prices should be monitored, too. In your daily newspaper, there are three figures quoted, the first two indicating the price. The bid quote is a discounted yield that a dealer is willing to pay—the annualized discount from par or the face value. The ask quote is the same thing—the annualized discount from par that the seller is offering. But it's the third figure—the yield, or annualized rate of return, also called the "coupon equivalent"—that's the key figure. This is the actual rate of return you will receive by holding the bill to maturity, and this is the figure you should use when comparing yields of alternative investments.

But, again, even that is not an absolute yield. Because T-bill quotes are taken at different times during the trading day, the yield shown in the newspaper does not necessarily reflect the last T-bill trade of the day.

To figure the actual worth of T-bills on a given day takes a little arithmetic (but just a little). You multiply the face value of the T-bill times the offer rate (expressed as a percentage), times the days remaining until maturity, and divide the resulting figure by 360 days. Subtract that figure from $10,000 and you find out the amount of cash you will have to put up to buy the bills. Again, the price appreciates as you get closer to maturity. A 5 percent six-month T-bill might be priced at $9,686 per $10,000 of face value. That same T-bill three months later—three months closer to maturity—might sell for $9,813.

Let's summarize and strategize. T-bills have amazing flexibility as an investment. Unlike certificates of deposit, where being locked into a maturity can cost you missed opportunities, T-bills can be turned into cash in a secondary market. T-bill yields are tax-advantaged. Comparing a 5 percent T-bill with a 5 percent CD is really no comparison. The T-bill's income or price appreciation is not subject to state or local taxes, and for a taxpayer in the 5 percent state income bracket, the T-bill's equivalent yield is 5.26 percent.

From a pure investment and financial planning strategy standpoint, T-bills always make more sense than certificates of deposit. For example, many investors buy T-bills that are due April 15 in order to have the cash to pay their income tax obligation. But with a lot of demand for the same T-bill, the price soars, pushing the yield down. A smarter move is to buy a usually lower priced/higher yielding T-bill that matures after April 15, sell it before the IRS deadline day and put the proceeds into a money market mutual fund for four days. Chances are, you'll realize a profit, and you'll have the cash when you need it.

The trick with treasury bills, as with any treasury security, is to know their strengths and shortcomings. Indeed, bankers, brokers, and other financial salespeople market CDs as convenient and safe. But for anyone willing to stack them up side by side with a treasury bill and weigh the pluses and minuses before they commit their capital, the choice is clear.

6

TREASURY NOTES: MORE RISK, MORE REWARD, STILL SAFE

Treasury notes are aimed at investors who are willing to lend money to the U.S. Government for more than a year so it can meet its financial obligations. Treasury notes are identical to treasury bills in two important ways: the principal—the money loaned or invested—is guaranteed to be redeemed 100 cents on the dollar if the notes are held to maturity, and the income earned by noteholders is not subject to state and local income taxes.

Indeed, there is absolutely no credit risk on these federal debt instruments, and the only tax obligation on income is to the U.S. Government.

But there are several crucial differences between treasury notes and treasury bills. First, T-notes have stated coupon interest that pays holders cash twice a year. Because treasury securities are now issued in book-entry form, coupons are not attached. For those bond holders that have physical bonds with coupons attached, the Fed is encouraging them to transfer the certificates to book-entry form and to no longer clip coupons. Since most banks do not cash U.S. Treasury coupons, they must be taken to a Federal Reserve Bank or branch. With T-bills, the interest is factored into the discounted price and is paid at maturity.

Second, you have a greater choice of maturities with T-notes than with T-bills and the minimum purchases are considerably lower. Historically, treasury notes were issued in maturities ranging from two to ten years with face values as low as $1,000 per note. However, while the minimum purchases officially remain the same, the four-

and seven-year maturities have been scrapped. Indeed, the last time the treasury issued a $1,000 T-note with a maturity less than four years was in 1986. That T-note today belongs on a wall, as a framed antique, not in an investment portfolio. Today, the $1,000 minimum for treasuries is for a five-year maturity or longer.

Usually, the Treasury auctions off T-notes in denominations of $5,000 increments, but they also come in $10,000, $100,000, and $5 million denominations. The auctions are held on a strangely staggered basis; three-year and ten-year notes are auctioned quarterly—on the first week of the second month. The two- and five-year T-notes are auctioned monthly. But three years ago, the Treasury switched to what it calls a Dutch auction for the two- and five-year T-notes. This benefits investors who put in a non-competitive bid because they often get the single highest yield. When the government auctions the three- and ten-year maturities, the yields vary, and you could get one of the lower yields.

You can also buy T-notes through the government's TREASURY DIRECT plan, as described in Key 5, or from Federal Reserve banks and their branches and pay no fees or commissions. (Forms for tenders: PD 5174-1, a buff color, for 2- and 3-year notes and PD 5174-3, white, for 5- and 10-year notes.) Plus, you can write a personal check for T-notes through TREASURY DIRECT instead of a cashier's check. Or you can purchase T-notes in the secondary market through a brokerage firm and resell them back to the firm when you want to cash out.

Who are the prime customers for treasury notes? I've found that banks are the big buyers, although individuals and managers of small portfolios favor them because they can deliver a slightly higher yield in exchange for going out a little further on the maturity scale.

Nevertheless, T-notes have the same great flexibility and liquidity of T-bills and T-bonds because they, too, can be sold before maturity into that very active secondary market. The flip side of the coin is that investors can go into that secondary market and buy a T-note, again through a brokerage firm, with only three months to maturity, avoid price fluctuations, have access to ready cash, and perhaps earn a greater rate of return than by owning a T-bill.

However, that strategy really works only for investors with a tremendous amount of cash—$1 million or more. The reason: institutions generally buy those close-to-maturity higher yielding notes. On top of that, the brokerage fees on those T-notes would offset the higher yields—which means that smaller investors who want to stay short should stick with T-bills.

T-notes also have their own personality. They are not callable. Generally, that means the Treasury cannot retire the debt before maturity at terms that are favorable to the U.S. Government and thereby shortchange investors. This is a king-sized advantage treasuries have over corporate bonds, and its importance shouldn't be downplayed. Companies issuing bonds with call features will retrieve them out of investor hands without warning if interest payments on the high yield are squeezing their cash flow or if the company feels it can issue new bonds with lower interest rates.

7

T-NOTES FOR
INCOME INVESTING

Treasury notes can be an excellent financial planning tool for hold-to-maturity investors looking for a steady stream of interest for up to ten years at a yield generally above T-bill rates.

But it is impossible to talk in absolutes. There are some facts of life—and investing strategies—that most investors are not aware of when it comes to treasury notes. Understanding them will give you the edge over other investors.

First, once a treasury note is issued, there is no way to tell whether it is a T-note or a T-bond except by its maturity. (T-notes, as mentioned earlier, have a maximum maturity of 10 years.) People are either "bill" investors or "bond" investors; there are very few, if any who consider themselves "note" investors. The term "T-note" merely reflects the fact that these are mid-range government securities. Even the newspaper quotations each day do not differentiate between a T-note and a T-bond in their tables.

Second, depending on your financial objectives, you can buy a T-note selling for a premium—above par (or face value)—and often get a higher current yield. Why? Because so-called "premium notes" carry coupons with greater-than-market rate interest, hence they often sell for more than 100 cents on the dollar. More income, but little or no capital appreciation.

Buying a high coupon or premium T-note is actually a wise defensive strategy if you are bearish on the bond market. If interest rates do go up, you realize more income to reinvest at higher rates. Plus, the high yield of a premium T-note cushions a price fall when interest rates climb. Why? Because the higher yield throws off more investment dollars, and those notes are in demand. Premium T-notes have shorter durations and are less volatile. (Duration is the average life of the cash flow of the T-note. Because the interest payouts are higher, that shortens the average life of the cash flow, hence the shorter duration.)

At the other end of the spectrum, a solid strategy for bond market bulls is to buy a low coupon or discount treasury note. Because these T-notes have coupons paying at less than the market rate, they sell at a discount, sometimes a deep one. In addition, the older the issue, the wider the bid and ask spread, making these notes less liquid, less easily traded. Hence, the demand for them is lower. But when interest rates drop, discounted T-notes surge in price. If you hold to maturity, you may realize less coupon income, but there's greater capital appreciation.

Meanwhile, there are some other yardsticks used by sophisticated T-note investors. Patrick Retzer, portfolio manager of Heartland U.S. Government Securities Fund in Milwaukee, likes to see a "sustained premium" between a T-note yield and the rate of inflation. Typically, he says, T-note yields should be three percentage points over the inflation rate. "That's a real interest rate over and above inflation, and that's what you really earn," notes Retzer.

Retzer also advises investors to make their T-note purchases just before or after an auction. Here are some reasons why. Usually, Wall Street has a tendency to push up yields right before an auction to enhance greater participation by institutional investors. Or, right before a Treasury auction, institutions will want to get into the newest treasury security, so they will often sell the treasuries they bought at a prior auction to generate liquidity. This is especially true for the two-year T-note, which is auctioned monthly. Such unloading floods the market with a stream of these maturities, and the oversupply of these older issues often depresses their prices and creates buying opportunities for astute investors. "Plus, on the five-year T-note, 85 percent of the time we get a rally after a five-year Treasury auction," adds Retzer.

At the same time, newly auctioned treasuries in the most popular maturities—two to five years—command a premium because of their liquidity. So, if the oversupply of the existing two-year T-notes causes them to sell at a premium, it's your chance to capitalize on one of the most venerable economic theories—an imbalance of supply over demand pushes down price. That's your chance to pounce.

Retzer studies the yield curve intently when selecting T-note maturities. "A flat or inverted yield curve is an excellent time to buy ten-year T-notes."

Still, the Heartland portfolio manager's savviest strategy is to "build a ladder of treasuries" that include some two-, five-, and ten-year maturities. This reduces the average maturity and spreads out the interest rate risk. "If interest rates move up dramatically, the two- and five-year T-notes will not be as adversely affected as the ten-year T-note," says Retzer. "It has an averaging effect."

Indeed, Retzer, who keeps his Heartland U.S. Government Securities Fund portfolio well stocked with treasury notes, is a real fan. "T-notes are the most liquid higher yield securities in the world. They're exempt from local and state taxes, and that can be a nice kicker for residents of high-tax states—probably accounting for another one quarter percent interest equivalent which only helps the yield."

8

THE SAFETY OF A TREASURY INSTRUMENT

For generations, the treasury bond was a granite-like symbol of security that arrived as an ornately engraved certificate suitable for framing but was normally kept in a safe-deposit box. This was the ultimate U.S. Government IOU, a loan to the Treasury Department for 30 years, guaranteed to be repaid with interest in the form of semiannual coupon payments. The T-bond was as good as gold. Better, in fact, because it paid a yield.

It is still a rock-solid investment, yet it has changed somewhat with the times. Treasury bonds, with the longest maturity and usually the highest yield compared with other treasury securities, are no longer issued in bearer form. The engraved certificate, known better as a bearer bond, was expensive to produce and difficult to replace if lost. Bearer bonds, the equivalent of cash, are too cumbersome to handle. Plus, holders of bearer bonds must detach or clip the coupons and redeem them for cash at a Federal Reserve Bank or one of its branches (most commercial banks no longer cash them)—a hassle in today's world, where time is a precious commodity. In 1982, bearer bonds were phased out, although there are plenty that have not yet matured and are still in circulation.

All treasuries, including T-bonds, T-notes, and T-bills, are now issued in book-entry form. Instead of issuing certificates to investors, these securities are now electronically logged as accounting entries with the U.S. Treasury, a Federal Reserve bank, a financial institution, or some other custodian. There is no coupon-clipping with book-entry form. Interest and maturity payments are made automatically, directly deposited into your checking or brokerage account, and the Fed encourages physical bondholders to exchange certificates for book-entry securities. This is a huge, high-tech step forward from even the "registered form" of issuance when the owner's name was typed on the face of the T-bond or T-note.

Fundamentally, though, the T-bond remains the same. It is issued in denominations as low as $1,000 and in increments as small as $1,000 and as large as $5 million. There is a single maturity—30 years—hence it's known as the "long bond." Like T-bills and T-notes, the coupon interest on T-bonds is exempt from state and local income taxes, but is subject to federal income tax. (Of course, realized gains from any price appreciation must be reported as income on federal and state returns.)

T-bonds, like T-bills and T-notes, can also be purchased at auction through the Treasury Direct program at no cost. You make a noncompetitive bid, which means you accept the price and interest rate established by the auction. To buy direct, you submit a "tender" (a gold-colored form number PD 5174-4) and payment to one of the twelve Federal Reserve Banks or one of its branches, or directly to the Bureau of Public Debt in Washington. Mailed bids must be postmarked no later than the day before the auction date and received prior to the issue date. To avoid snags, it's wise to mark the envelope "Tender for Treasury Bonds" in the bottom left corner of the envelope.

Newly auctioned T-bonds are also sold by commercial banks, usually for a flat fee of $25 to $50, or bought through investment brokerage firms.

In reality, comparatively few individual investors buy treasury bonds at auctions these days and sock them away for three decades without touching them. In today's world, most yield-sensitive buy-and-hold investors are going toward shorter maturities to maximize their coupon income. Savers who want to lock up high rates generally lean toward bank certificates of deposit because they're considered convenient. Yet, the long-term CD is absolute folly because you lose liquidity and flexibility the minute you put your money away.

Instead, if you are a saver wanting a high yield to maturity and the assurance of total safety, you should not overlook the 30-year T-bond, and there is one very good reason for this: you can sell out in an instant if you need the money, and you pay no early withdrawal penalties, those expensive fees usually levied by banks and savings and loans for breaking into a certificate of deposit before maturity. If you sell your T-bond in the secondary market, you'll pay a commission and be in a cash position within minutes. Indeed, the liquidity of the secondary market for T-bonds is as appealing to savers and investors as the Treasury Department's guarantees of zero credit risk.

Nevertheless, that strategy is not without financial risk. To liquidate T-bonds before maturity, you must sell them into the secondary market at the current bid price—a price that may be less than the price you paid. The 30-year T-bond, being at the extreme end of the yield curve, is subject to greater market risk than any other treasury security. When interest rates move, the price of a 30-year T-bond will fluctuate more than the price of a one-year T-bill. Why? Because the extended maturity makes a basis point worth more the farther out you go on the yield curve. (See Key 12 on the yield curve.)

9

THE MOST VOLATILE TREASURIES

The thirty-year treasury bond can experience price swings so severe that few individual investors trade it. I personally stay with intermediate treasuries like the five-year T-note to minimize price volatility. Or I will trade T-bond futures on the Chicago Board of Trade. (See Key 17.)

Who, then, buys the long bond and for what reason? Perhaps 95 percent of the players in the T-bond market are institutions that possess the steel nerves needed to withstand the price fluctuations and have long-term financial obligations to meet. The big buyers of thirty-year bonds are life insurance companies and pension funds; both have to deliver cash at some future date and T-bonds, bought and held to maturity, are an asset that offsets that liability.

In addition to guaranteed return, institutions that need a long-term debt instrument do not have to worry about having a treasury called away before maturity. Unlike corporate bonds, including even AAA-rated corporates, most T-bonds have a noncallable provision.

Other T-bond buyers are primary dealers who may strip off their coupons and resell them as zero-coupon bonds to investors who want to use them to fund Individual Retirement Accounts (IRAs), Keogh Plans for self-employed individuals, and other tax-advantaged (qualified) retirement plans. Additional buyers include portfolio managers of mutual funds holding U.S. Government securities. Banks generally buy treasuries when their loan volume sags, but they usually stick with shorter maturities. Banks would rather forgo a few basis points in yield to avoid the price volatility of the longer bond.

Even investors who do not buy the long bond watch it like a hawk. Its yield to maturity is considered to be the prevailing long-term interest rate. That's why it is often called the "benchmark bond"; it reflects the true cost of money.

There are some important characteristics and behavioral traits of the newly issued thirty-year T-bond that every investor should know. For openers, the newest issues are usually the most actively traded and are called "on-the-run" bonds. Spreads between their bid and ask prices are often two to four basis points lower than a comparable, older T-bond because investors are paying for liquidity. As the T-bond ages, it's referred to by the number of years remaining before it matures: an original thirty-year bond with five years to go before the Treasury must redeem it becomes a "five-year bond."

The thirty-year T-bond is, however, a favorite of the very aggressive trader looking for leverage. You can buy long bonds on margin for about 10 percent down with the brokerage firm financing the balance but retaining physical possession of the bonds as collateral. Leveraging the volatile thirty-year T-bond is a risky strategy. If interest rates move up sharply, the price of bonds will drop just as quickly. If the value falls significantly, you may be forced to ante up more cash within a few days. Or the brokerage firm may sell you out of your position, and you could lose part or all of your original cash down payment.

Portfolio managers look at the thirty-year treasury bond with real respect. If you're a long-term investor, "it is the best way of locking in a rock solid stream of income without the danger of having it called away," says Ian MacKinnon, senior vice-president and head of the fixed-income division of Vanguard Group of Investment Companies, the giant mutual fund family. Backed by the U.S. Government, "it has no credit risk and in virtually every state, the income is exempt from state income tax," he adds.

"From a market risk viewpoint, though," warns MacKinnon, "it is incredibly risky." He says the thirty-year T-bond will fluctuate 11 to 12 percent in price for every 1 percent change in interest rates. The 200 basis point increase in long bond interest rates from late 1993 to late 1994—from 5.80 percent to 7.80 percent—produced a 22 percent decline in the price of the bonds themselves. "There is no efficient way to protect yourself from the ravages of a sharp increase in interest rates other than by liquidating the bond or short-selling a treasury futures contract or shorting a T-bond itself. Any of these maneuvers would be difficult for an individual investor to do." Indeed, individual investors who are unwilling to accept the volatility of the T-bond should steer clear of them. Contends MacKinnon: "It is virtually impossible for you to time the market so well that you can hedge the downside risk on a treasury bond and capture all the upside income potential."

MacKinnon notes that the Treasury's recent decision to reduce the auction of the thirty-year treasury bond from quarterly to twice a year hasn't been a plus or a minus for investors. "There has been a very moderate reduction in the supply of long bonds, but the marginal positive offset on interest rates has been offset by negatives—such as fears of inflation."

Still, investors pursuing a high yield and who can stomach the volatility should consider a mutual fund instead of buying the individual T-bond. Vanguard has two mutual funds with portfolios that are 100 percent invested in treasury bonds. Both have an average maturity of 21.1 years. MacKinnon says the funds' performances are either at the top or bottom of the performance rankings—they are that volatile. "But for an investor approaching retirement, concerned about credit quality and interested in a high, stable stream of income, or for a person setting money aside for a child's college education, they can make sense."

Indeed, most professional traders do not advise individuals to buy the thirty-year T-bond for anything less than a hold-to-maturity strategy simply because it requires constant monitoring. Even professional portfolio managers will only use the long bond judiciously. "Typically, bond fund managers will always have some long bonds in a sector of the portfolio," says James Bianco, research director of Arbor Trading Group in Barrington, Illinois, which works closely with institutional bond managers. "If they're bullish (expecting interest rates to drop), they will hold more long bonds. If bearish (expecting rates to rise), they will hold less."

But Bianco is strongly opposed to unseasoned investors even buying a T-bond mutual fund for its high yield. It's simply too volatile. "You can get the same total return owning a five-year treasury note as you can owning a bond fund," he contends. "And here's why. You can buy the five year T-note direct from the Fed free instead of paying a load or management fees with a bond fund. And you can always sell it through any broker if you suddenly have to get rid of it."

He is adamantly opposed to individual investors buying T-bonds in small amounts through a brokerage firm, insisting they are prohibitively expensive from a commission standpoint. Individual investors would likely pay half a percent of the face amount, while institutions with their purchasing power and clout as repeat customers get those wafer-thin commissions of $\frac{1}{64}$ to $\frac{1}{256}$ of a percentage point.

The bottom line on the T-bond? There are dozens of trading strategies on how and when to use them. But unless you have at least $100,000 to commit to the long bond, the time, expertise and steel-plated stomach to pick off the profits while riding out roller-coaster price fluctuations, stick with shorter maturity treasuries. The extra yield usually generated by the volatile long bond isn't worth the anxieties when your own money is at risk.

10

ZERO-COUPON GOVERNMENTS: THE PROS AND CONS OF "STRIPS"

Zero-coupon bonds, at first blush, sound like a worthless investment. If there is no coupon, hence no yield, why would anyone invest solely for the potential of price appreciation?

The fact is, zeros pay no income during the life of the bond, but there is an interest rate quoted and a payoff—when the bond matures. In fact, because there is no coupon attached to the bond, and no periodic interest payments, zeros sell at a deep discount from par. So, when you couple the guaranteed price appreciation with principal paid at maturity, the gains can be whopping.

First, a little background. Zero-coupon bonds can be corporates, treasuries, or municipals. In all cases, the dealer has taken a conventional bond and stripped it of its interest coupons. The difference is that zero treasuries—unlike corporates and munis—have no credit risk. Just like a normal T-bond, they are backed by the full faith and credit of the U.S. Government. They come in denominations as low as $1,000 (but since they're discounted, they sell for far less) and, like regular T-bonds, are issued in maturities that go out as far as thirty years.

In recent years, zero or "stripped" treasuries have acquired some exotic names. Wall Streeters normally call them STRIPS, an acronym for Separate Trading of Registered Interest and Principal of Securities. (STRIPS was actually created by the Treasury Department and the Federal Reserve Bank.) Earlier, Merrill Lynch trotted out TIGRs, short for Treasury Investors Growth Receipts. Lehman Brothers followed with LIONs (Lehman Investment Opportunity Notes), while Salomon Brothers started selling CATS (Certificate of Accrual on Treasury Securities).

Regardless of what they are called, zero treasuries have one drawback: investors pay income tax each year on the accreted interest (the annual increased value). In other words, while you are not collecting any coupon income, you're taxed on that year's prorated appreciation.

As a result, investors should only consider zero treasuries as an investment for a tax-free or qualified plan. That's one reason that pension funds and other institutional-sized tax-exempt investors have been big fans of zero treasuries. Individuals can accumulate them in Individual Retirement Accounts (IRAs) and Keogh Plans to avoid paying income tax on the income realized that year and on any price appreciation. However, they will pay federal and any applicable state taxes when they retire and withdraw the funds.

Apart from being taxed along the way until maturity, zeros have another failing. Indeed, zero treasuries are almost identical to T-bills in one big respect: they sell at a discount, pay no interest, and principal isn't paid until they mature and are cashed in. Like T-bills, you can sell zero treasuries before the maturity date because there is an active secondary trading market with plenty of liquidity.

So, you see, zero or stripped treasuries are like a double-edged sword. One edge has this enticing, enormous guaranteed profit owing to the deep discount from the face value. For a one-time cash payment of $190, a stripped treasury with 8.5 percent interest rate is guaranteed to mature at $1,000 in 20 years.

The other edge of the sword requires you to pay taxes on "phantom" income every year. Yet, if interest rates climb, you have no coupon income to invest at the higher levels as you would with a conventional bond. In short, to collect your coupon income, you have to hold to maturity for your lump sum payoff.

11

STRIPPED TREASURIES: SHOPPING HARD BEFORE YOU BUY

In the past, zero or stripped treasuries had some alluring benefits that often persuaded investors to hold to maturity. At one point, zero treasury yields were slightly higher than couponed bonds, and during the years of double-digit interest rates investors could lock in some towering rates and tax-deferred income. Second, old tax laws allowed investors to use zeros to fund a college education for their children.

In those days youngsters, regardless of age, were taxed according to the level of their own income. Obviously, this placed most children in a rock-bottom bracket, and parents had to make only minimal cash outlays at tax time. But when the Tax Reform Act of 1986 was passed, the new law said that youngsters under 14 were to be taxed at their parent's bracket; at 14 or over, they were to be taxed according to their own income. That threw a monkey wrench into a great strategy: buying zero-coupons with staggered maturities for a newborn. That way the first bond would mature in eighteen years to coincide with the child's freshman year in college, and the remainder matured in the three successive years, just in time to make tuition payments.

The concept is still valid. It's known on Wall Street as "matching liabilities"—creating a lump sum of cash to meet a massive payment, and some people are still using zeros as a forced-saving strategy to underwrite the cost of college while paying the taxes along the way. That may work for a teenager 14 and up if parents feel a zero treasury makes economic sense after taxes. However, anyone with extremely young children might want to explore Series EE Bonds (see Keys 25 and 26) where there are new tax benefits for what are called "education bonds."

Nevertheless, zero treasuries still have enormous appeal to a variety of investors. Most of them are the large, institutional variety, says Mark Mahoney, vice-president and a zero-coupon bond trader and analyst with Donaldson, Lufkin & Jenrette, the New York investment firm. "The institutional market is very vibrant with insurance company investment managers, for example, using them to fund payoffs thirty years out, or mutual fund portfolio managers using them for trading strategies."

Mahoney says the institutional market for stripped treasuries "dwarfs" the retail or private investor market, but he agrees the bonds are an intelligent way to "fund your child's college education or any future liability." As he explains it, "if you buy a regular bond, you get coupon payments all year long and you have to reinvest the income in an uncertain interest rate environment. When you buy a twenty-year strip, you know exactly what you get in year twenty."

The Donaldson, Lufkin & Jenrette zero specialist does not advise private investors to trade zeros for fast profits. "The thirty-year zero-coupon treasury is two-and-a-half times more volatile than the regular (couponed) treasury bond"—which, itself, has volatile price gyrations in response to interest rate fluctuations.

Another Wall Street zero-coupon expert says private investors who want to "buy and sell or actively trade instead of hold to maturity will get their eyes ripped out by the brokers who will load up the quote with various fees, markups and commissions." A favorite ploy among some brokers is to tell a zero-bond customer that there is no commission when there really is, but it's just hidden. A commission, technically, is an up-front sales charge. However, the brokerage firm's institutional trading desk usually just adds a markup to the net price of the bond, and the customer is none the wiser.

To be on the safe side, shop around. Get at least five different quotes from five brokers, and you will be amazed at the variance among zero prices because some brokerages have zeros in inventory while others have to buy from a government bond dealer. As for commissions, while they should never be more than 1 percent of the face amount of the zero treasuries, hopefully they will actually be only one quarter of 1 percent. Ask the broker to break out the cost and the commissions or extra costs. And if you're told the purchase is commission-free, you can bet the broker is being compensated with a credit, often one eighth of 1 percent, back from the trading desk.

This is also an opportunity to find out if your broker is actually working on your behalf. Zero treasuries are not a commonly requested investment, and if you are told your broker can't really get you the best offering and you are pointed to another source—don't be surprised. The pros operate that way and you'll know you have a person looking out for your net worth.

There are some specific investment strategies that work well with zero or stripped treasuries. For instance, if you think interest rates will rise over the next ten years, buy one zero coupon bond due in five years. When that matures, buy another five-year zero, which hopefully will be at a higher rate.

But if you expect interest rates to be volatile but trending downward in future years, a so-called "long strip"—a thirty-year zero T-bond—will often outperform a thirty-year couponed T-bond in its rate of return on your money; long strips sell at a very steep discount from face value. On the other hand, a strategy for bears is to buy a one- or two-year "short strip" and remain liquid for reinvestment purposes.

12

HOW THE YIELD CURVE CAN SET YOU STRAIGHT

The yield curve is a great decision-making tool for people investing in U.S. Treasury securities. But it is also a difficult concept for investors to grasp because there are no ironclad rules for interpreting the curve. The yield curve is probably best described as a fairly reliable barometer for predicting the price risks—and rewards—in holding government securities to their maturity date.

Until recently, the yield curve didn't command that much attention except from bond portfolio managers, traders, and other institutional investors. But with the avalanche of new hedge funds—very aggressive risk takers—and more investors using sophisticated techniques to reduce their risk, the yield curve has become a critically important and newly popular decision-making tool.

"Betting on the direction of interest rates is a risky venture for any investor," says Jurrien Timmer, who manages the U.S. fixed-income department for ABN AMRO Securities in New York, an investment banking unit of Holland's largest bank. Instead, one way of lowering the risk taken on an outright interest rate bet is by "putting on a yield curve trade." Essentially, this involves taking a view on the shape of the yield curve rather than betting on the absolute direction of interest rates.

For instance, says Timmer, a trader might short-sell some two-year T-notes and "go long a duration-weighted equivalent in thirty-year bonds. In doing so, the trader bets on the relative direction of rates while remaining 'duration neutral.'" Because a bond's duration, or sensitivity to changes in interest rates, increases with its maturity, a yield curve trade that is duration neutral "involves selling more two-year T-notes relative to the number of thirty-year T-bonds that are purchased," Timmer explains. "As a result, the negative duration of the short position would exactly offset the positive duration of the long position, leaving the trader with no outright risk in terms of the absolute duration of rates."

Timmer concedes "there are risks," and the main risk of a yield curve trade lies in "being on the wrong side of the trade." However, he says, "If the trade is managed properly, the main risk will be less than the risk involved in being wrong on an outright interest rate bet."

Where do you find this important barometer for bond investors? You will find a yield curve for treasuries in the *Wall Street Journal* and *Investor's Business Daily* but probably not in your local newspaper. Yet it can be drawn, or plotted, based on the quotations found in the table headed "Treasury Bonds, Notes and Bills" in your newspaper's financial section. Now, before we chart our yield curve and make our investment decisions, let's recall some truisms for fixed-income investments.

It's generally believed that prices fluctuate more on debt securities with longer maturities. No one can forecast the future, but investors willing to buy a thirty-year bond should theoretically be compensated for tying up their money for a long time, enduring price volatility, and gambling on the creditworthiness of the instrument itself. Will that debt instrument pay off the holder at maturity?

With a U.S. Treasury security—a T-bill, note, or bond—one worry is eliminated. Treasuries theoretically have no credit risk because they're backed by the full faith and credit of the U.S. Government. But holders still face the same risk of fluctuating prices as interest rates themselves change. Our principal risk is price fluctuation and that largely depends on interest rates—whether the Federal Reserve is pumping money into the economy or tightening the flow—and investor expectations.

To construct your own yield curve, plot the current on-the-run issues on the horizontal axis of a graph and the yields on the vertical axis. The exact securities that qualify as "on-the-runs" change as new bonds, notes, and bills are issued, although the standard maturities are generally three months, six months, one year, two years, three years, five years, ten years, and thirty years.

The yield curve graph on the next page is based on numbers reported in the *Wall Street Journal* on September 23, 1994, and shows a positive slope.

In plotting these yields on a piece of paper, you will see a yield curve that slopes upward, or positively. Why? Because short-term interest rates are generally lower than long-term interest rates. This rising yield forecasts the additional income you will make taking the extra risk of owning T-notes with a longer maturity. The challenge for investors is to find that one point on the curve where they feel comfortable with the yield from the treasury note (or bill) without sensing they are locked in and unable to take advantage of more attractive yields offered by other treasury issues—whether bills, bonds, or notes.

But the wild card in plotting the yield curve and making investment decisions is investor expectations. A positively sloped yield curve says the prevailing opinion is that interest rates will climb in the future, but investors mistakenly buy long-term treasuries for the fattest yield. Instead, they should be buying the short-term bonds and rolling them over at maturity—renewing them at a higher yield.

The secret is to look out on the horizon of a positive yield curve, regardless of how steep it becomes, and find the point where you get maximum return with minimum worry.

But not all yield curves slope positively. When short-term interest rates are higher than long-term rates, that usually indicates the market is expecting interest rates to decline sometime in the near future. These fears or expectations produce a negatively sloping or inverted yield curve. When this happens, investors generally buy the shortest maturities, again hoping to grab the highest yields. Once again, they are making a mistake and should be buying intermediate or longer-term maturities.

Sample Yield Curve (as of 09/22/94)

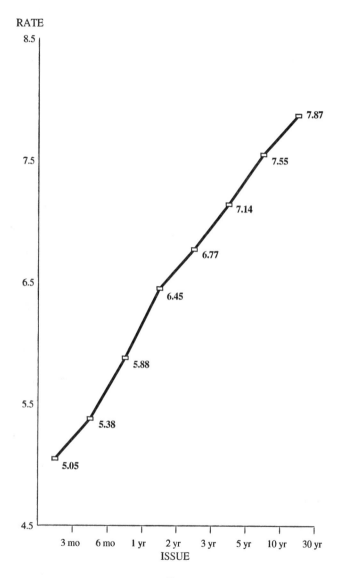

RATE

8.5

7.87

7.55

7.5

7.14

6.77

6.45

6.5

5.88

5.5

5.38

5.05

4.5

3 mo   6 mo   1 yr   2 yr   3 yr   5 yr   10 yr   30 yr
ISSUE

Why? Because both of the gut reactions—investing in long maturities in the face of a positive yield curve and looking short-term when the curve turns negative—are what I call "herd instinct" mistakes. Everyone starts galloping toward what appears to be the same refuge and the market outfoxes them at maturity. When it comes time for rolling over your money into the more attractive yields, you won't find them available. In a positively sloped yield curve, you're locked into a lower yield, and your money isn't available to take advantage of the higher rates. Indeed, experience has taught me that when the obvious appears to be the smartest choice, it's wise to go in the opposite direction.

The yield curve can also be flat. That means short-term interest rates are almost equal to long-term rates.

To summarize, expectations—what the market thinks is going to happen to interest rates—produce a horizontal (flat) yield curve when interest rates are stable, an upward-sloping yield curve when interest rates are low, and a downward-sloping yield curve when interest rates are high.

It's a mistake, though, to picture the yield curve as static—negative, positive, or flat. The curve is constantly moving because treasuries trade almost twenty-four hours a day. For example, an inverted yield curve that is starting to lose its inversion is usually a bullish sign heralding rising bond prices. Why? Short-term rates are starting to fall relative to long rates, thus indicating an easing of monetary policy by the Federal Reserve Board. And when rates drop, both prices, moving inversely, climb. Essentially, the market is changing its attitudes, perceptions, feelings, and inflationary expectations and is looking for deflation.

The flip side of the coin is just as dramatic. When the positively sloped yield curve starts to lose its steepness, short-term rates rise. The market is anticipating the Fed will tighten the faucet on the money flow. Borrowing subsides, and inflation fears take hold.

The bottom line? The yield curve is not a fail-safe forecaster of how treasury prices will perform. But it is probably the best yardstick you have for maximizing your yield while maintaining your liquidity before a bond matures.

13

HOW TO FIND A BOND BROKER

Not all investment brokers are alike. Stockbrokers, often called "account executives," are supervised by a sales manager and usually must generate a certain commission income quota. Hence, the stocks they recommend are often part of a brokerage firm's inventory—shares their firm may have underwritten or their research department is recommending. Account executives must move that stock.

A good stockbroker is rarely a specialist in treasuries or the fixed-income market. It is virtually impossible to be an expert in both stocks and bonds. Bond brokers usually have a broader grasp on global markets and world economies, and they must be skilled in forecasting the direction and behavior of short- and long-term interest rates. Interest rates, as I've said earlier, drive the price and yields of treasuries and all fixed-income securities.

Bond brokers have no market tape to follow to track up-to-the-second trades, and instead work from a series of screens. For that reason, you must make sure that any broker you choose to work with has access to these Telerate or Bloomberg screens. Otherwise, your broker will lag the market and your executions will suffer.

There are also differences among bond brokers. Those who work for large investment houses, like stockbrokers, are usually advised by their management to sell from their inventory. They rarely shop the street to track down the precise treasury instrument at the exact rate, maturity, and price to fit the client's need. It is the investment business equivalent to buying off the rack.

However, an independent bond broker with no ties to any major brokerage organization is free to shop other firms—that is, other broker/dealers—to see what they have in their inventories and what the price may be. Because prices, commissions, and markups vary, it is important to find an energetic broker who will work on your behalf—even if it takes shopping five or six other firms to track down the best transaction for you.

Finding a good bond broker is not that easy. First, find a broker who is a successful investor for his or her own account. That's right. You want to work with someone who does not see you as a source of income, a new commission-generating account. Of course, brokers are not so benevolent that they work without compensation, but you don't want them to be living off your portfolio either. Ask the general manager of a brokerage firm near you: "Who is the most successful bond broker in your office?"

Avoid the "broker of the day" system wherein new account executives are assigned the walk-ins (or the call-ins).

Next, arrange a meeting. There are several things to look for, and you'll spot them or feel them ten minutes after you arrive at the broker's office. Find out if he or she is organized and backed up with a support staff to handle clerical requests from you or your accountant. Your bond broker should also take the time and interest to pass along information such as articles, rulings, and research that can help you in your investment decision-making.

Is the personal chemistry right? Does this broker make you feel comfortable? Are your questions encouraged or simply tolerated? Is there any arrogance in the broker's voice?

Now comes question-and-answer time. And *both* of you should ask some probing questions. Find out whether prospective brokers have put their own money on the line and have followed their own recommendations. Ask for client references as well and check them out. Look for long-term relationships. Has the broker been in the business at least ten years, through good markets and bad?

Expect brokers to ask you some rather penetrating questions, too. Are you conservative or aggressive? Trying to build capital or generate income? What are your current investment and personal financial goals? The best brokers will try to see exactly where you stand on the risk/reward spectrum so they can tailor investment advice exactly to your personal objectives. Do they answer your questions thoroughly? How do they react when you ask about commissions, markups, fees? The better brokers will take the time to walk you through a transaction, explaining it every step of the way. Will they refer you to top-performing, no-load mutual funds even though they reap no commission?

Remember, you are not marrying your broker. If the relationship is not working, end it, and move on to another one. After all, it's your money.

14

HOW TO READ THE FINANCIAL PAGES

The financial pages of any major newspaper serve up a buffet of information to the investor who wants to track treasuries as well as other economic market trends.

Locate the quotation table of treasury bonds, notes, and bills and begin by examining the first three columns for a full description of the security you are considering. As an example, the first column of the table on the next page shows a 6½ percent note of Aug 97 which means a $1,000 note will pay $65.00 annually, or 6½ percent × $1,000.

The second and third columns give the maturity date of the bond or note by month and year; when two or more years are listed here, it means the security matures on the later date but could be called (or redeemed) by the Treasury as early as the first date, in order to reissue the debt at a lower coupon if market rates drop. If there is an "n" listed after the month, the security was issued as a note; a "p" indicates that the note is exempt from withholding tax if bought by a nonresident. The fourth and fifth columns quote the prices that buyers were bidding and sellers were asking on the date for which the statistics are listed. These prices are quoted in 32nds for bonds and notes and in 100ths for bills and reflect a percentage of par (or $1,000 value) for the security. In other words, for that same 6½ percent note due in August 1997, at the close of trading on Thursday, September 22, buyers were bidding 99%2 of par value ($1,000 × 0.992812 = $992.81) while sellers of that security were asking for 99¹¹⁄₃₂ ($1,000 × 0.993437 = $993.44).

The sixth column reflects the change in bid price, again expressed in 32nds for bonds and notes and in 100ths for bills, from the prior day's close.

The final column lists the yield to maturity.

TREASURY BONDS, NOTES & BILLS

Thursday, September 22, 1994

Representative Over-the-Counter quotations based on transactions of $1 million or more.

Treasury bond, note and bill quotes are as of mid-afternoon. Colons in bid-and-asked quotes represent 32nds; 101:01 means 101 1/32. Net changes in 32nds. n-Treasury note. Treasury bill quotes in hundredths, quoted on terms of a rate of discount. Days to maturity calculated from settlement date. All yields are to maturity and based on the asked quote. Latest 13-week and 26-week bills are boldfaced. For bonds callable prior to maturity, yields are computed to the earliest call date for issues quoted above par and to the maturity date for issues below par. *-When issued.

Source: Federal Reserve Bank of New York.

U.S. Treasury strips as of 3 p.m. Eastern time, also based on transactions of $1 million or more. Colons in bid-and-asked quotes represent 32nds; 101:01 means 101 1/32. Net changes in 32nds. Yields calculated on the asked quotation. ci-stripped coupon interest. bp-Treasury bond, stripped principal. np-Treasury note, stripped principal. For bonds callable prior to maturity, yields are computed to the earliest call date for issues quoted above par and to the maturity date for issues below par.

Source: Bear, Stearns & Co. via Street Software Technology Inc.

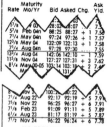

GOVT. BONDS & NOTES

Rate	Maturity Mo/Yr	Bid	Asked	Chg.	Ask Yld.
4	Sep 94n	99:31	100:01	....	1.12
8⅜	Sep 94n	100:02	100:04	−1	1.00
9½	Sep 94n	100:08	100:10	−1	3.33
4¼	Oct 94n	99:30	100:00	−1	4.18
6	Nov 94n	100:05	100:07	....	4.29
8½	Nov 94n	100:15	100:17	....	4.19
10⅛	Nov 94	100:24	100:26	....	3.97
11⅝	Nov 94n	100:30	101:00	−1	4.05
4⅝	Nov 94n	99:30	100:00	−1	4.38
4⅝	Dec 94n	99:26	99:28	....	5.05
7⅝	Dec 94n	100:19	100:21	−1	4.99
8⅝	Jan 95n	101:01	101:03	....	4.86
4¼	Jan 95n	99:21	99:23	−1	5.05
3	Feb 95	99:02	100:02	....	2.83
5½	Feb 95n	100:01	100:03	....	5.22
7⅞	Feb 95n	100:29	100:31	−1	5.14
10½	Feb 95	102:00	102:02	−1	4.99
11¼	Feb 95n	102:09	102:11	−1	4.99
3⅞	Feb 95n	99:12	99:14	−1	5.20
3⅞	Mar 95n	99:06	99:08	−2	5.38
8⅜	Apr 95n	101:18	101:20	−3	5.35
3⅞	Apr 95n	99:00	99:02	−1	5.49
5⅞	May 95n	100:05	100:07	−2	5.52
8½	May 95n	101:26	101:28	−1	5.47
10¾	May 95n	102:31	103:01	−1	5.47
11¼	May 95	103:18	103:20	−2	5.39
12⅝	May 95	104:20	104:24	....	4.96
5⅛	May 95n	99:00	99:02	−1	5.55
4¼	Jun 95n	98:26	98:30	....	5.57
8⅞	Jul 95n	102:14	102:16	−1	5.65
4¼	Jul 95n	98:24	98:26	....	5.71
4⅝	Aug 95n	98:30	99:00	−1	5.80
8½	Aug 95n	102:09	102:11	−1	5.75
10½	Aug 95n	104:02	104:04	−4	5.67
3⅞	Aug 95n	98:07	98:09	....	5.80
3⅞	Sep 95n	98:00	98:02	−1	5.88
8⅝	Oct 95n	102:23	102:25	....	5.86
3⅞	Oct 95n	97:25	97:27	−1	5.94
5⅞	Nov 95n	99:02	99:04	−1	5.93
8½	Nov 95n	102:23	102:25	−1	5.94
9½	Nov 95n	103:27	103:29	−1	5.90
11½	Nov 95n	106:02	106:06	....	5.80
4¼	Nov 95n	98:00	98:02	−1	5.98
4¼	Dec 95n	97:26	97:28	....	6.02
9¼	Jan 96n	103:27	103:29	....	6.09
4	Jan 96n	97:08	97:10	....	6.11
7½	Jan 96n	101:23	101:25	−1	6.10
4⅝	Feb 96n	97:30	98:00	−1	6.15
7⅞	Feb 96n	102:07	102:09	....	6.13
8⅞	Feb 96n	103:17	103:19	−1	6.13
7½	Feb 96n	101:25	101:27	....	6.13
5⅛	Mar 96n	98:14	98:16	−1	6.18
4¼	Mar 96n	96:20	102:08	....	6.17
9⅜	Apr 96n	104:17	104:19	−1	6.23
5½	Apr 96n	98:26	98:28	....	6.25
7⅜	May 96n	102:00	102:02	....	6.25
4¼	May 96n	96:26	96:28	....	6.28
7⅞	May 96n	101:20	101:22	−1	6.27
9¾	May 96n	99:09	99:11	....	6.29
5⅞	May 96n	102:02	102:04	+1	6.30
6	Jun 96n	99:13	99:15	....	6.32
7⅞	Jun 96n	102:16	102:18	....	6.32
7⅞	Jul 96n	102:16	102:18	+1	6.35
6⅜	Jul 96n	99:11	99:13	....	6.40

Rate	Maturity Mo/Yr	Bid	Asked	Chg.	Ask Yld.
4⅝	Sep 96n	100:31	101:01	....	6.45
8	Oct 96n	102:27	102:29	+1	6.47
6⅞	Oct 96n	100:20	100:22	+1	6.52
4⅞	Nov 96n	95:22	95:24	−1	6.54
7¼	Nov 96n	101:12	101:14	....	6.52
6½	Nov 96n	99:28	99:30	....	6.53
6⅛	Dec 96n	99:05	99:07	....	6.50
8	Jan 97n	102:30	103:00	....	6.58
6⅛	Jan 97n	99:07	99:09	....	6.59
4⅜	Feb 97n	95:29	95:31	+1	6.60
6½	Feb 97n	100:07	100:09	....	6.62
6⅞	Mar 97n	100:16	100:18	+1	6.63
8½	Apr 97n	104:07	104:09	+1	6.65
6⅞	Apr 97n	100:14	100:16	+1	6.66
6½	May 97n	99:15	99:17	....	6.70
8½	May 97n	104:08	104:10	....	6.69
6¾	May 97n	100:01	100:03	....	6.71
6⅜	Jun 97n	99:08	99:10	....	6.65
8½	Jul 97n	104:13	104:15	+1	6.72
5½	Jul 97n	96:26	96:28	+1	6.72
5⅞	Aug 97n	99:09	99:11	+1	6.75
8⅝	Aug 97n	104:25	104:27	....	6.75
5⅜	Sep 97n	96:30	97:00	+1	6.77
5½	Sep 97n	96:17	96:19	+1	6.77
8⅞	Oct 97n	105:07	105:09	+1	6.80
5¾	Oct 97n	97:00	97:02	....	6.82
8⅞	Nov 97n	105:20	105:22	....	6.83
6	Nov 97n	97:18	97:20	+1	6.84
7⅞	Jan 98n	102:27	102:29	....	6.88
8⅛	Feb 98n	96:07	96:09	+1	6.89
8⅛	Feb 98n	103:21	103:23	+1	6.88
5⅛	Mar 98n	94:17	94:19	....	6.92
5⅛	Mar 98n	94:13	94:15	+1	6.93
7⅞	Apr 98n	102:27	102:29	+1	6.94
5⅛	Apr 98n	94:07	94:09	+1	6.95
9	May 98n	106:14	106:16	+2	6.95
5⅛	May 98n	94:26	94:28	....	6.98
5⅛	Jun 98n	93:27	93:29	+1	6.99
8¼	Jul 98n	104:03	104:05	+1	6.99
5⅛	Jul 98n	94:03	94:05	+1	7.01
9¼	Aug 98n	107:15	107:17	+1	7.00
4¾	Aug 98n	92:08	92:10	....	7.02
4¾	Sep 98n	92:03	92:05	....	7.03
7⅛	Oct 98n	100:10	100:12	....	7.02
4¾	Oct 98n	91:27	91:29	+1	7.05
3½	Nov 98n	91:21	92:21	+1	5.51
8⅞	Nov 98n	106:13	106:15	+1	7.05
5⅛	Nov 98n	92:31	93:01	+1	7.08
5⅛	Dec 98n	92:27	92:29	+2	7.08
6⅛	Jan 99n	97:13	97:15	+2	7.08
5	Jan 99n	92:08	92:10	+1	7.09
8⅞	Feb 99n	106:19	106:21	+2	7.08
5⅛	Feb 99n	94:03	94:05	+2	7.06
5⅞	Feb 99n	95:07	95:09	+1	7.12
6½	Apr 99n	99:16	99:18	+1	7.11
6½	Apr 99n	97:16	97:18	+1	7.11
9⅛	May 99n	107:25	107:27	+2	7.11
6¼	May 99n	98:12	98:14	+1	7.15
6¾	Jun 99n	98:10	98:12	+1	7.16
6⅞	Jul 99n	96:27	96:29	+1	7.15
6⅞	Jul 99n	98:23	98:25	+1	7.18
8	Aug 99n	103:14	103:16	+1	7.14
6⅞	Aug 99n	98:23	98:25	+2	7.17
4¾	May 96n	95:02		2	7.17
	Apr 99n		102:38	1	7

Maturity

Rate	Mo/Yr	Bid	Asked	Chg.	Ask Yld.
7⅞	Aug 04n	103:01	103:07	+1	7.51
7⅜	Feb 04n	88:25	88:27	+1	7.50
5⅞	May 04n	97:24	97:26	+1	7.57
12⅜	May 04	132:09	132:13	+1	7.58
7¼	Aug 04n	97:28	97:30	....	7.55
13¾	Aug 04	142:16	142:10	−	7.59
11⅝	Nov 04	127:27	127:31	+3	7.62
8¼	May 00-05	103:14	103:18	+2	7.60
	May		131		
8	Nov	100:2	00:2		7.9
7¼	Aug 22	92:17	92:19	+5	7.9
7⅞	Nov 22	96:25	96:27	+6	7.91
7⅛	Feb 23	91:09	91:11	+5	7.87
6¼	Aug 23	81:17	81:19	+5	7.87
7½	Nov 24	96:22	96:24	+5	7.78

U.S. TREASURY STRIPS

Mat.	Type	Bid	Asked	Chg.	Ask Yld.
Nov 94	ci	99:11	99:11	−1	4.74
Nov 94	np	99:11	99:11	−1	4.76
Feb 95	ci	98:01	98:01	−1	5.19
Feb 95	np	98:00	98:01	−2	5.24
May 95	ci	96:20	96:21	−2	5.45
May 95	np	96:19	96:20	−3	5.49
Aug 95	ci	95:06	95:07	−2	5.60
Aug 95	np	95:04	95:05	−2	5.68
Nov 95	ci	93:19	93:20	−2	5.89
Nov 95	np	93:18	93:18	+2	5.93
Feb 96	ci	91:30	91:31	+2	6.13
Feb 96	np	91:28	91:30	+4	6.17
May 96	ci	90:10	90:12	−2	6.29
May 96	np	90:10	90:11	+4	6.30
Aug 96	ci	88:29	88:30	−2	6.31
Nov 96	ci	87:06	87:07	−2	6.50
Nov 96	np	87:04	87:06	−4	6.53
Feb 97	ci	85:17	85:19	−2	6.63
May 97	ci	83:30	84:00	−2	6.73
May 97	np	83:30	84:00	−2	6.73
Aug 97	ci	82:13	82:15	+2	6.80
Nov 97	ci	82:11	82:14	−2	6.81
Nov 97	ci	80:25	80:27	−2	6.89
Nov 97	np	80:26	80:0	−2	6.89

TREASURY BILLS

Maturity	Days to Mat.	Bid	Asked	Chg.	Ask Yld.
Sep 29 '94	3	3.95	3.85	−0.12	3.90
Oct 06 '94	10	4.15	4.05	−0.04	4.11
Oct 13 '94	17	4.18	4.08	−0.07	4.14
Oct 20 '94	24	4.25	4.15	−0.04	4.22
Oct 27 '94	31	4.23	4.19	−0.06	4.26
Nov 03 '94	38	4.40	4.36	−0.03	4.44
Nov 10 '94	45	4.53	4.49	+0.03	4.58
Nov 17 '94	52	4.55	4.51	−0.01	4.60
Nov 25 '94	60	4.59	4.57	−0.01	4.67
Dec 01 '94	66	4.65	4.63	....	4.73
Dec 08 '94	73	4.72	4.70	−0.02	4.81
Dec 15 '94	80	4.76	4.74	−0.02	4.86
Dec 22 '94	87	4.79	4.77	....	4.89
Dec 29 '94	94	4.79	4.77	−0.01	4.90
Jan 05 '95	101	4.86	4.84	−0.01	4.97
Jan 12 '95	108	4.88	4.86	....	5.00
Jan 19 '95	115	4.91	4.89	....	5.04
Jan 26 '95	122	4.96	4.94	+0.01	5.09
Feb 02 '95	129	5.01	4.99	+0.01	5.15
Feb 09 '95	136	5.04	5.02	+0.01	5.19
Feb 16 '95	143	5.05	5.03	....	5.20
Feb 23 '95	150	5.07	5.05	....	5.23
Mar 02 '95	157	5.10	5.08	....	5.27
Mar 09 '95	164	5.15	5.13	+0.03	5.33
Mar 16 '95	171	5.18	5.16	....	5.36
Mar 23 '95	178	5.19	5.17	....	5.38
Apr 06 '95	192	5.26	5.24	+0.01	5.46
Apr 20 '95	220	5.31	5.29	....	5.52
Jun 01 '95	248	5.35	5.33	−0.01	5.59
Jun 29 '95	276	5.39	5.37	....	5.62
Jul 27 '95	304	5.44	5.43	−0.01	5.70
Aug 24 '95	332	5.51	5.49	....	5.79
Sep 21 '95	360	5.55	5.53	−0.02	5.85

Understanding the role that treasury securities play in your portfolio often hinges on a few mathematical formulas. Some are too complex to walk through here, but others are simple to grasp and implement. (For reference purposes, the long bond, 7½ percent of November 2024, as listed in the September 23, 1994 *Wall Street Journal,* is used for these examples.)

The following calculation will give you the approximate yield on T-notes or T-bonds selling below or above par. If they sell at par, the coupon rate and the current yield will be the same.

$$\text{Current Yield} = \frac{\text{Coupon Payments}}{\text{Market Price}}$$

$$= \frac{\$\ 75.00}{\$967.00}$$

$$= .0775$$

$$= 7.75\%$$

$$\text{Approximate Yield to Maturity} = \frac{\text{Annual Coupon Payment} + \left(\begin{array}{c}\text{Face Market} \\ \text{Value} - \text{Price}\end{array}\right) \bigg/ \begin{array}{c}\#\text{years} \\ \text{to maturity}\end{array}}{(\text{Face Value} + \text{Market Value})/2}$$

$$= \frac{\$75.00 + (1{,}000 - 967.50)/30}{(\$1{,}000 + 967.50)/2}$$

$$= \frac{\$75.00 + \$32.50/30}{\$1967.50/2}$$

$$= \frac{\$\ 76.08}{\$983.75}$$

$$= 7.73\%$$

For treasury bills, the following calculations will help you understand how these discount securities may fit your investment needs. (For reference purposes, the bill due December 22, 1994, is used for the following calculations.)

Discount $= \dfrac{\dfrac{\text{Ask price} \times 10{,}000}{100}}{360} \times \text{Days to maturity}$

$= \dfrac{\dfrac{4.77 \times 10{,}000}{100}}{360} \times 87$

$= \dfrac{477}{360} \times 87$

$= \$115.28$

Discount Rate (Yield) $= \dfrac{\text{Discount}}{\text{Par value}} \times \text{Time multiplier}$

$= \dfrac{\$115.28}{\$10{,}000} \times \dfrac{360}{87}$

$= .011528 \times 4.14$

$= .0477$

$= 4.77\%$

Yield to Maturity $= \dfrac{\text{Discount}}{\text{Purchase price}} \times \text{Time factor}$

$= \dfrac{\$115.28}{\$9{,}884.72} \times \dfrac{365}{87}$

$= .01166 \times 4.20$

$= .0490$

$= 4.90\%$

15

BUILDING A CONSENSUS VIEW OF THE MARKET

If you do not plan to hold treasuries to maturity but want capital appreciation, your wisest investment strategy may be to form your own consensus view of the market. Your goal is to anticipate just what the market is expecting from certain key economic indicators before the numbers are announced. This takes doing enough homework on the economy to develop your own personal hunches. It is exactly the way the seasoned professionals invest.

Or you can even buy a consensus from various full-time market watchers and use it to help shape your hunches and decisions. A Northbrook, Illinois, company called MBH Commodity Advisors provides a daily consensus on 32 markets for $39 a month. While it covers stocks and commodities, it also has a consensus of professional traders and investors on fixed-income securities ranging from conservative treasury bills to the volatile thirty-year treasury bond.

Ironically, the vision behind these market consensus reports—he calls it the Daily Sentiment Index—does not blindly follow his own findings. "The majority of my clients are professional traders," says Jake Bernstein, president of MBH Commodity Advisors and publisher of *MBH Weekly Commodity Letter*, "yet some investors are leery of the sentiment index because they think it represents herd thinking." But Bernstein's strategy is to identify the "majority opinion"—the consensus—"then do the opposite." Why? Because he feels consensus or sentiment precedes changes in market direction by several days.

Bernstein, who surveys as many as 100 people daily to compile his sentiment index, cited, as an example, a recent T-bill reading that was 93 percent. More than nine out of ten felt that T-bill futures were going up and yields would drop. "Consensus is an expectation and 90 percent of the investors had already taken action, so there was no power to fuel that market move any more." His hunch: park cash in T-bills because yields were going up.

Clearly, no consensus—or interpretation and investment strategy—is foolproof. For example, Leonard Santow, managing director of Griggs and Santow, New York City financial consultants specializing in capital markets and publisher of *Griggs & Santow Report*, tells of a time the nonfarm payroll employment figures were announced, only to be "much weaker than what the market expected." That was good news for investors long in the thirty-year T-bond because it rallied immediately. But some investors—those who felt the market was anticipating solid numbers and who were short the long bond—were hurt. As Santow so accurately puts it, "the market has an estimate" on virtually every number, every statistic that affects the bond market. The serious, active investor cannot afford to ignore this fact of life.

Santow doesn't put much faith in market consensus reported in newspapers. "That might be twenty or thirty people and Wall Street may not care about their opinion. Wall Street is much more interested in the opinions of a smaller, select group of people with a well-known track record—Salomon Brothers, J.P. Morgan, ourselves, Reid, Thunberg." Santow says even numbers out of Washington don't move markets as expected. He tells of a one-time gain of 179,000 in employment statistics that pushed the price of the thirty-year bond up a point. "This was a kneejerk reaction—off consensus—and major traders wanted to sell so the bond price increase didn't last."

But here is the wild card that can cause grief to the casual investor in treasuries, or to the person who does not pay attention. The same sets of statistics released monthly in Washington does not always move or dominate the market every month. In fact, as economic cycles evolve, the market, investors, and the press seem to shift their attention from one set of statistics to another, often without explanation.

Not long ago, the ballooning trade deficit was being heralded as the blasting cap that would reignite inflation. As a result, all eyes and ears were on the merchandise trade deficit announced each month by the Commerce Department. These figures reflected the growing U.S. trade deficit with Japan, dramatically driving home the point that America was buying far more goods from Japan than our big trading partner was buying from us. The trade deficit was seen as a major drain on the strength and worldwide vitality of the U.S. dollar, and that had negative connotations for the bond market. As the trade gap began to widen with each announcement, the bond market reacted sharply and treasury prices fell.

Within six months, though, the dollar was a nonstory, the markets were no longer placing that much importance on the trade deficit, the financial press didn't consider it major news, and its impact on bond prices the day that the figures were announced was reduced.

This points to yet another problem facing treasury investors who diligently try to keep informed and to read the market. The U.S. Government securities market is like one big county fair shooting gallery. Wooden ducks crisscross before your eyes on a high speed track. Each duck is an important source of information. But once you've drawn a bead on a plump duck, it disappears from sight.

Yet the fastest, surefire way to lose money in treasuries is not by pouncing on or ignoring every statistic or trend that is perceived to nudge prices in one direction or the other. The death knell is arrogance. When you think the bond market should be reacting one way and it's doing the exact opposite, never fight it. Do an about face and go with the flow.

This is probably the greatest argument of all for setting aside some time during your week to take a good look at bond market behavior regardless of whether your money is in funds or short-term maturities or locked up for the long haul. You want to stay a step ahead.

Is it really worth the trouble? "A consensus can be dangerous because it gives investors a false sense of security," asserts Lakeshman Achuthan, associate research economist at Columbia University's Center for International Business Cycle Research, which publishes the *Early Economic Outlook,* a newsletter analyzing business and inflation cycles. Instead of trying to predict impact of a government statistic and how it will move the market—where everyone is looking at the same number— Auchtman's center "looks for turning points in the business cycle. We believe the real profit opportunities are being on the right side of the business cycle."

Yet one of the most respected bond market watchers, Jim Grant, who pens *Grant's Interest Rate Observer,* says "Yes, you should know what is going on the world. But under no circumstance should a lay investor collect points of view and attempt to fade them (go the opposite way) in a misguided attempt to practice the art of contrary opinion."

No one said consensus-building is a cakewalk, but remember these principles: the market doesn't react well to good economic news and prices can only go down. The market reacts positively to bad economic news and treasury prices generally go up. (Unless, of course, market expectations have already anticipated and discounted those moves.) By anticipating the market, you won't get trampled when investors make the wrong call. Because people who have to get out of their positions quickly—whether short or long—will rush to break the door down, the market gyrates. If more people learned how to monitor the news that moves the treasury markets and anticipate how they will react, U.S. Government securities would be an even safer place to be.

16

GOVERNMENT AGENCY BONDS: MORE YIELD, LESS LIQUIDITY

Ask a hundred investors what leaps to mind when you mention U.S. Government securities, and you can bet 95 percent will sing out treasury bills, bonds, and notes. Treasuries are clearly the investment choice for people who want to enjoy rock-solid safety or to speculate on interest rate movements.

One big reason? The Treasury has a powerful public relations machine, known as great word of mouth, working on its behalf. Although some people mistakenly think bank certificates of deposit are the highest yielding, most bulletproof investment of all, the majority of conservative and adventurous investors know treasury bills, bonds, and notes are the only securities in the world today that have zero credit risk; they are backed by the full faith and credit of the U.S. Treasury. A bank CD? It is guaranteed only by the Federal Deposit Insurance Corporation, an agency of the U.S. Government.

There is a difference, although it's a slight one. Uncle Sam stands behind the obligations of the federal agencies that have been created essentially to make the country function more efficiently. So far, he has never let any agency default on its debts. But "agencies" do not have the ironclad Full Faith and Credit guarantee that makes their word 100 percent worry-free. One exception: the Financial Assistance Corporation (FACO) bonds, created to bail out the farm credit system. FACO bonds are guaranteed by the Secretary of the Treasury.

In years past, investors who could live with a tad more risk have put their money into the coupon securities issued by these Federal agencies and have been rewarded handsomely. After all, the Federal Home Loan Bank (FHLB), the Federal National Mortgage Association (FNMA), and the Federal Farm Credit Banks (FFCB), among other agencies, have had to raise money for a variety of reasons, ranging from buying Government-guaranteed mortgages to helping keep farm families solvent. And to convince investors to buy their IOUs instead of credit risk-free T-bills or T-bonds, agencies had to pay a higher coupon yield.

Another reason agencies sold at premium compared to treasuries was the bad press they received in the mid-1980s when the Federal Farm Credit Banks were plagued with a rash of bad loans. More recently, a rising tide of thrift industry failures has caused concern over debt instruments issued by the Federal Home Loan Bank. But, again, no one has lost a nickel from a default.

However, agencies have market risk. They behave like any other bond—prices rise when interest rates drop (and vice versa)—and commissions are slightly higher, but there is no fixed level. Most agencies are bought and sold by primary dealers marketing with institutions—pension funds, government bond mutual funds, and other fixed-income portfolio managers who want to squeeze every last basis point out of a transaction. Conventional brokers account for only an estimated 15 to 20 percent of the market for agencies today. That's no big surprise. Creditworthiness aside, they are not the same great deal they once were.

Here's why. We're now in the mid-1990s and the 100-plus basis point premium government agencies once enjoyed over treasuries has shriveled to about 35 points for fixed-rate securities depending on where you are on the yield curve, says Howard Glicksman, vice-president and senior agency trader for Smith Barney in New York City. Fixed-rate, non-callable agency bonds with ten-year maturities trade 28 to 30 basis points over ten-year T-notes. Agencies with callable provisions could trade 60 to 80 basis points over a comparable ten-year fixed-rate T-note. The callable feature is a risk for investors, and the market compensates them for it with a higher payout.

Agencies no longer deliver a towering yield compared to intermediate and long-term treasuries; investors are not being paid huge sums for the risk of leaving a debt instrument guaranteed by the U.S. Treasury in favor of one deemed an "obligation" of the U.S. Government. Glicksman has some investment strategies for agency investors: "If you're looking to buy and hold, buy the individual agency bond because you can always get out of it easier. But you've got to pay attention to the market. If you want to let someone else pay attention for you, you might be able to get a higher yield on a basketful of agencies (a mutual fund)."

Second, the market for agencies does not have the same liquidity as the treasury market. Generally, treasuries are auctioned in $10 billion amounts, and agencies are underwritten in lots of $300 million to $800 million and sold by investment banking firms. Hence, with a smaller supply and institutional demand, the spreads between the bid and ask prices available to individual investors are much wider than for treasuries. For example, an on-the-run ten-year treasury note had a spread of $\frac{1}{32}$ to $\frac{2}{32}$ between bid and ask at the same time a ten-year Fannie Mae bid/ask spread was $\frac{2}{32}$ to $\frac{4}{32}$. Says Glicksman: "The market has gotten a lot more efficient."

Federal Home Loan Bank, Federal Farm Credit Bank, Tennessee Valley Authority and, in some states, Student Loan Marketing Association all have local and state income tax exemptions on income earned. Some agencies are not exempt from state and local taxes. Investors have mistakenly bought agency securities and, after paying state taxes on the coupon interest, netted less than a comparably priced treasury note.

Finally, always look at the bottom line, not the big upfront number. Government bond mutual funds, which are often packed with agencies to beef up the yield, may promise better returns than a pure treasury mutual fund. By subtracting the higher management fee of the government bond fund and adding the tax advantages of the all-treasury mutual fund, the safest route may also be the most profitable.

Bid, ask, and yield quotations on U.S. Government agency issues are found in most daily and financial newspapers. The local and state tax-exempt status of these bonds varies from state to state, so be sure to check with your local tax professional:

Federal Farm Credit Bank
Federal Home Loan Bank
Federal Home Loan Mortgage Corp. (Freddie Mac)
Federal National Mortgage Association (Fannie Mae)
Financial Assistance Financing Corp. (FACO)
Government National Mortgage Association
  (Ginnie Mae)
Inter-American Development Bank
Residential Funding Corporation (Refco)
Student Loan Marketing Association (Sallie Mae)
Tennessee Valley Authority
World Bank

17

TREASURY FUTURES: UPPING THE ANTE ON RISK AND REWARD

The word "leverage" is the investment community's term for a world-class balancing act. Imagine supporting a hippopotamus—nose first—on the palm of your hand. Keep it in the air long enough and you'll win accolades and applause. But if the beast suddenly makes the wrong move, you can be crushed.

Financially speaking, leverage is the great multiplier. Use leverage, and you multiply your reward—and your risk.

Treasury futures are, quite possibly, the most highly leveraged investment strategy of all. For $5,000, you can control $1 million worth of treasury bills. That's the equivalent of buying the T-bills with one-half of 1 percent down and not having to make payments. But remember that you own nothing. What you purchase is a futures contract—an agreement to buy a $1 million T-bill at a specific price on some future date. The margin payment, that one-half of 1 percent, is nothing more than a good faith deposit.

Futures contracts generally—and treasury futures specifically—have one king-size advantage over other leveraged investments such as buying stocks and bonds on margin. A margined purchase requires you to pay cash for a percentage of the total price and to borrow money and finance the balance. Then you must pay interest on the money borrowed—even though you can often write it off as an expense against any profits. But the point is, you are on the hook for the total face value of the investment.

With any futures contract, treasuries included, you do not borrow a dime to buy the contract. The good faith deposit buys nothing except control over a huge block of the commodity you promise to buy at that specific date—in this case the $1 million in T-bills. But, remember, those T-bills are only yours temporarily. And you are responsible for their behavior.

Now here is where the excitement of leverage comes into play. You can buy treasury futures of varying maturities on bills, notes, and bonds, but if you are convinced the rate of inflation is going to decline slowly over the next six months, you probably want to go out long on the yield curve.

And there you have a choice. You can either buy $25,000 worth of thirty-year T-bonds and pay $25,000 cash. Or you might put the same $25,000 into a T-bond fund that holds the thirty-year treasury. Why? Because the thirty-year T-bond most closely tracks the rate of inflation. Or, if this were April, you could buy a T-bond futures contract due in June. For a deposit of $2,200, or 2.2 percent, you would control $100,000 worth of the thirty-year. For a cash outlay of one-tenth of what it would cost to buy $25,000 worth of T-bonds, you get four times as many bonds.

Treasury bond futures contracts move in increments of $\frac{1}{32}$ of a percentage point, commonly called a tick, just like the actual treasury bonds. Each tick is worth $31.25 per contract, so a 1.0 point move up in price equals $1,000 per contract. Now, that would be no big deal had you shelled out cash to buy the $100,000 of T-bonds, but since you put up only $2,200 for the contract, you make a 45 percent return on your money in just a few days. That's the magic of leverage—the potential of a huge return for a tiny investment.

But the flipside of this huge gain is not so rosy, warns Michael Krauss, managing director of technical strategies at Chemical Securities, Inc., a subsidiary of Chemical Bank. This may be a drastic but not an extraordinary example. "If you make a bet that a government unemployment or inflation figure will be low and hence friendly for the market, and it comes out high, and therefore, very unfriendly, it's conceivable the T-bond price could fall a point and a half to two points over a couple of days," Krauss explains. If it was two points, you would lose $2,000 or almost your total equity—the cash deposit you put up on that contract.

Worse yet, futures exchange regulations require you to keep $2,000 on margin, so you would get a call to come up with another $1,800 within 24 hours or you'd have to liquidate and lose the contract and the balance of your deposit. "In the huge bear market in bonds in 1994, this scenario was all too prevalent," he adds.

This is not even a severe situation, according to Krauss. The thirty-year T-bond perched out there on the end of the yield curve, is extremely volatile. So it is no surprise that a futures contract of $100,000 in thirty-year T-bonds would experience the same sharp swings on very good and very bad news. In an extreme case, theorizes Krauss, you could have $5,000 in cash supporting a T-bond futures contract and an exaggerated disruption in the marketplace—a war breaks out, a world leader is slain—that knocks 3.5 points off the price of the T-bonds you own. That's a $3,500 loss in a matter of a couple of days. You would get a call for another $700 to bring you back to the $2,200 required deposit to allow you to margin futures. But here's a case where you should take your losses and not answer the call.

First, to lose $3,500 means that both you and your broker were asleep at the switch. In the case of a war, a skilled bond broker should have realized that scores of technical indicators were flashing red. Shooting wars are rarely spontaneous. Pressures build. Plus, futures exchanges have limits on how far up or down a contract price can move in any given day. With T-bond contracts, the limit is three points up or down in any one trading day. Hence, to lose three and a half points over two days means your broker didn't pull you out when the blood started flowing.

Some professionals think that regular investors have no business rolling the dice with treasury futures. Norm Zadeh, who rates and selects money managers nationwide and publishes *Money Manager Verified Ratings*, insists that only one person in a thousand really makes money trading futures contracts. "People are led to believe they can make money competing in the commodities market against extremely well capitalized, extremely intelligent, extremely well researched professionals like (legendary trader) Paul Tudor Jones, gold producers, coffee growers, and pig farmers who have a huge advantage for all the reasons above. The fact is, even the pros have a lot of trouble making money consistently in the futures market."

18

LIMITING RISK WITH FUTURES

The most fundamental strategy in treasury futures is to build a floor to limit your downside risk before even thinking about going through the roof. On highly leveraged investments, it's human nature—call it optimism or, better yet, greed—to think that even if you're only a little bit right, a small amount of cash can produce mammoth returns.

That's looking down the wrong end of the gun barrel. Instead, make sure your bond broker has studied the technical charts and can tell you where bond prices have hit support levels on interest rate hikes in the past. There is no guarantee that history will repeat itself exactly, but this intelligence can help you and your broker set your stop losses. Stop losses are price levels that you and your broker set up as circuit breakers of sorts. If your futures contract falls to that level, it automatically trips that circuit breaker, and your position is liquidated.

There is tremendous leverage in treasury futures, so an investor should only buy a contract after he determines where the price support levels are. "That's when you set your stop loss orders and you do it religiously," says Bill Gary, president of Commodity Information Systems, Oklahoma City, publishers of *Price Perceptions*. Stop losses can minimize risk and maximize returns. "Once that point is hit and you're 'stopped out,' you're free of your market bias and you can stand back and make an objective decision whether you want to go back in again," adds Gary. To limit your downside, pick a point where you'll feel the pain. You must know when to say you're wrong.

While some commodity traders set "ticks" ($\frac{1}{32}$ of one price point or $250 per $100,000 of futures contracts),

Gary advises investors and his staff to "set stop losses on treasury futures contracts using a dollar amount—I've got $1,000 to risk"—or pick specific prices. For instance, if a bond is trading at par or 100, he might set a "support point" at 98, the point we know we want to get out. "If rates go up and the T-bond falls below 98, we're out."

Again, there are different ways to automatically exit the market and manage your risk. Besides the stop loss order, there is a market order that can be a buy or sell order at a current price. A limit order is another way to activate a buy or sell when the bond price hits a particular point, while a day order can automatically prompt a buy or sell if the price hits a particular point on a given trading day. When you figure that prices on treasury futures contracts can fluctuate in seconds, you can see how crucially important it is to stay on top of these markets.

Suppose the T-bond market is moving in your favor and your treasury futures contract is showing a profit? Gary puts in what are called "trailing stop losses." As the T-bond market advances toward his target price, say 102, he keeps raising the floor to, say $101^{20}\!/_{32}$. That way if interest rates appear likely to move up, Gary can instantly take his profit before he's stopped out.

Success in treasury futures involves more than having interest rates move in your favor. For openers, understand that futures are a speculation, not an investment. You do not hold the contract until the expiration date, unlike holding a bill or note to maturity. This means you are obligated to take what is called "physical delivery" of the T-bonds (or the bills or notes) and come up with the cash to pay for the full face amount of the contract. Usually, though, you sell out of the contract, hopefully at a profit, before it comes due. But you must also be able to stomach a loss and still sleep at night. Most brokerages would ideally like you to open a treasury futures account with $10,000 cash even though the deposit is only $2,200 for a T-bond contract. They would like to see this cash cushion because they know repeated margin calls may scare you out of the market. The only real rule of thumb—although it's a whiskered bromide—is "if it hurts you to lose or crimps your lifestyle, or both, don't risk your money."

Next, and I've said this over and over, you absolutely must have a firm conviction on which way interest rates and the economy are moving, and it doesn't always have to be bullish. Just as you can go short on individual treasuries if you think interest rates will rise and bond prices will fall, you can also go short on a treasury futures contract. But to have no opinion on the domestic markets and the economy or the world at large is a surefire recipe for disaster. The only thing worse is to try and buck the trend. If you get "stopped out" more than one day and you're looking—indeed, praying—for a turnaround, you can bet those prayers will not be answered. Take your losses, and next time set up a stop loss that automatically takes you out before it costs you too much money. Professional futures managers never risk more than 5 percent of their cash equity on any one trade.

Probably the best advice you can get on treasury futures is offered by Morris Markovitz, an astute commodity trader who publishes *Morry on the Market* in New York City. "Keep it simple." Realize that the size of the margin deposit is "no guarantee of performance and has no relationship to price volatility." Furthermore, according to Markovitz, "the more time and study you invest in treasury futures, the better you'll be paid for it." Indeed, that's a rather clever way of stating the most fundamental truths. And the dreaded flipside is just as valid. Put up your money and do no homework, and you'll pay the price—a big one.

Where do you go to study treasuries futures? You can start with the major commodity exchanges. The Chicago Board of Trade (CBT) trades T-note and T-bond contracts. The Chicago International Money Market (IMM) trades T-bill contracts. Other exchanges trade small contracts of assorted treasury futures, and all will send you extensive trading information. Overseas, T-bond futures contracts trade on the Sydney Futures Exchange, the Singapore International Monetary Exchange, and the London International Futures Exchange.

Different exchanges have different contract sizes, minimum movements, and trading hours. But don't worry about the technicalities. If you're going to up the risk/reward ante by going into treasury futures, make sure you have a skilled, seasoned futures broker, not some boiler-room operator who cold calls, promising immense returns. There are plenty of those characters around, and they have plucked many a pigeon.

Instead, find a commodities professional with a specific knowledge of treasury futures and let him or her be your mentor, says Woody Dorsey, publisher of *Bond Market Semiotics,* a weekly fax newsletter on the bond market published in Castleton, Vermont. "Treasury futures are a commodity, just like soybeans, and it's very dangerous for regular investors to play unless they have a resource—an advisor or consultant—who has expertise in this specialized market and can set guidelines for you," says Dorsey. "Remember, the professional investor is usually thinking and doing the opposite of what Joe Public is thinking and doing, and unless Joe has a smart specialist working with him, he will probably lose a lot of his money."

19

OPTIONS ON TREASURY FUTURES: WELCOME TO THE CASINO

If treasury futures move too quickly for you—and owning the individual T-bond or T-note does not provide you with the multiplying power of leverage—you have an option. Literally. You can buy or sell puts and calls on treasury futures and limit your exposure to huge losses if interest rates move suddenly and sharply against you. Welcome to the options casino.

Now options, specifically puts and calls, can be very confusing to first-time speculators. But let's clear the air. Options can be bought and sold on stocks, commodities, and treasuries. These are called "physicals," but options on the actual treasury security are not that liquid and should be avoided. The buying and selling of options on treasury futures contracts is a far more active and liquid market.

That's right. Options on treasury futures are a form of gambling, and you should only play if you are firmly convinced that interest rates will move one way or the other. No opinion or no time to formulate one? Steer clear of options, no matter how passionately your broker tries to interest you in them.

Treasury futures options, like any game, have their own ground rules and jargon. For starters, although they are traded in a secondary market—you can buy or sell them through your broker—they carry no guarantee that protects your principal. Indeed, if you buy options on treasury futures—either a put or a call—"you are likely to lose 100 percent of your money three out of four times," warns Robert Prince, manager of research and trading for Bridgewater Associates, a global fixed-income and currency management firm in Wilton, Connecticut and publisher of *Bridgewater Daily Observations*. "Then, one out of four times, you may recover what you lost, but over time you don't make money buying options. It's like putting money in a slot machine." Except that with a slot machine, you simply stuff in the money and pull the handle. Options require strategy.

A call option is a right, but not an obligation, to buy a treasury futures contract (the $100,000 T-bond contract traded on the Chicago Board of Trade, for instance) at a predetermined price, known as the strike or exercise price for a predetermined date, called the expiration date. The cost to buy the option is the premium. You would only buy a call if you thought interest rates would drop before the expiration date.

The opposite of a call option is a put. This is a way to bet that interest rates will climb and bond prices will fall and can be used as a vehicle to short a treasury futures contract. Buy a put option and you get the right, but not the obligation, to sell the contract at a specific strike price on or before a specific future date. Buying puts is a bearish strategy, so before you place that bet, you should have a keen sense that interest rates will soon move up.

"Essentially, you are buying insurance that interest rates will move in the direction you are anticipating," says Norm Zadeh, who also manages the annual U.S. Trading Championships. He, too, contends options writers or sellers have the upper hand in puts and calls because they have factored their risk into the price of the premium. Yet Zadeh is no fan of options on treasury bond futures in the first place. "Shorting a bond futures contract is better than buying a put or selling a call because the bid/ask spread in option transactions only makes the marketmakers rich."

Explaining a hypothetical transaction, Zadeh says, suppose an option has a value of 1.00 but buying the option could cost the investor 1.02 and selling the option might yield the investor 0.98. "The cost of getting in and out of the option is 4 percent and that doesn't include the commissions. If you're losing that much money every time you make an investment, it will make you poor in the long run."

With options, if you make a wrong call and hold the option until it expires, you've lost 100 percent of your call/put option premium by the expiration date. As a "wasting asset," it loses value every day; you hold it and do not exercise it. But you also have, pardon the expression, another option. If you realize you made a mistake and sense interest rates will move against you—up instead of down—you simply sell the call back into the options market. Naturally, if you hold it for even a day or two, you won't recover the full amount of your premium, but you won't lose the lion's share of it, either.

The only other way you can lose most or all of the premium is when interest rates do not move at all during the time you own your call. Why? Because the value wastes away while you wait to see some movement in rates, and it expires worthless. The majority of options do, in fact, expire worthless, accounting for the high percentage of losers.

Who is selling the call/put option you are buying? It may be an individual investor, but usually it's an institution. As the "option writer," the seller is betting either that interest rates will not budge or will move against you, the buyer. It's the seller who collects your premium and earns interest on it while you sweat until rates move or the option expires. Think of the seller as the casino; you, the buyer, are the gambler betting against the house. Sure, chances are very slim that you'll hit a jackpot—rates will drop or rise sharply, and you'll exercise your option to pocket a handsome profit by controlling the underlying treasury futures contract. But sometimes the casino loses, too.

Just don't bet on it. "The average person has no hope of winning," says Bruce Babcock, editor and publisher of *Commodity Traders Consumer Report* newsletter. "You know the odds are against you but, as a buyer, you never know how really big the odds are."

20

THE VIEW FROM ABROAD

"An investor in U.S. securities who is not following what is happening around the world," says Carl Weinberg, chief economist for High Frequency Economics, a New York City economic advisory firm, "is only playing with half a deck." The major financial institutions have a voracious appetite—and the up-to-the-second technology—to deal themselves a winning investment hand. Investors willing to take the global view can enhance their own returns—whether buying individual treasuries or mutual funds.

Ironically, Weinberg says there are no "hard and fast rules for cross-border investing" in U.S. Government securities. For the same transaction, one sophisticated investor may hedge the currency risk and stand only the market risk, while another equally skilled investor will not hedge at all.

In Japan, for example, yen-funded investors—they can be Japanese, American, or any nationality—are not buying the thirty-year treasury bond as they were three years ago because it's too volatile. "They are now making short-term trades in shorter-maturity treasuries, and they are hedging," says Will Lameyer, U.S. treasury bond trader with Lehman Brothers in Tokyo. "Yen-funded investors are buyers of U.S. Government securities when the dollar looks weak or is about to hit a near-term bottom because they know it will pop up, and they can take a profit quickly."

In the last two years, investing in U.S. treasuries has grown in the rest of Asia. Investors in China, Taiwan, Singapore, Hong Kong, and Malaysia are either actively trading—buying and selling quickly—or buying and holding, looking for the recently weak U.S. dollar to rebound. Both types of investors are important to the U.S. Government market. The speculators add liquidity to the market, while buy-and-hold investors add stability.

In England, investors are changing their views. Several years ago, one portfolio manager suggested the British "think of the world as being made up of fifteen interest rate markets, all independent economies with their own national problems and characteristics." But David Fuller, chairman of Chart Analysis Ltd. and editor of *FullerMoney* in London, disagrees. "We truly live in a global financial community—none of us exists in a vacuum—and the same bull and bear trends and fashion swings sweep across the bond markets worldwide." Fuller adds, however, that bull and bear cycles "overlap and have different leaps and lags," so investors have to do their homework and not just adopt one viewpoint.

Fuller says when the U.S. bond market was topping out in 1993–94 and the U.S. dollar was dropping against other currencies, "we were told we're in a slow-growth, noninflationary period where a bull bond market would extend indefinitely in every country. But when we saw the weakness in the bond markets firsthand in Germany, Japan, Australia, and the U.K., it was a much more compelling message. Think of it as a commercial. If we hear it once, it might not register. Hear it seven times and it sticks in our mind." Still, the U.K. has the world's largest holding of U.S. Government securities outside of America, bigger than Japan's, so its investment strategies should certainly be monitored. As of late 1994, with the weak U.S. dollar, many were taking a wait-and-see position, notes Fuller.

The Taiwanese who invest in U.S. Government securities are principally short-term investors who buy and hold treasury bills, often three-month maturities or up to two-year treasury notes, according to Doron Vidal, treasurer with China Trust Bank in New York. They do not buy treasuries for higher interest rates or safety of capital because Taiwan's own short-term government note and bank rates are two to three percentage points higher than those of the U.S. Government. Instead, they watch the foreign exchange or "forex" market. The dollar's relationship to other major currencies is a critical signpost because it's a tipoff to capital flows.

For example, if the Taiwanese expect the U.S. dollar to appreciate against the NT (New Taiwan) dollar, they will sell NT dollars and buy three-month T-bills. When the bills mature, they will collect the principal and interest and repurchase NT dollars. Remember, their original investment buys more NT dollars than it did three months ago. Again, they are betting on the currency, yet by investing in three-month T-bills, they don't have to worry about interest rate risk.

"A lot of overseas investments are based on family considerations," says Vidal. "Here, Chinese do want safety in one-year T-bills or two-year T-notes because the proceeds are going for a child's college education or a U.S. residence. They gamble at home in their own markets. Here they want safety and diversification." However, Chinese do not like mutual funds or managed accounts so, generally, you will not find them in U.S. Government bond funds. "Typically, they like to control their money and make their own decisions. They don't even mind losing as long as they have control."

21

MONITORING GLOBAL MARKETS CAN HELP INVESTORS AT HOME

One of Wall Street's shrewdest investors—Jim Rogers—who invests his own fortune around the world, insists it is critically important to know what foreign investors are thinking and doing when you are making investment decisions at home. Rogers, who retired at 37 after he co-formed the Quantum Fund, a global investment partnership that gained 4,000 percent in ten years, explains why: "Taiwan, Japan, mainland China and Germany have been investing in U.S. Government securities and accumulating huge stockpiles of dollars. If they ever stop, it could have a huge impact on our currency and the government bond market."

Rogers, who teaches finance at Columbia University and co-hosts CNBC's "Your Portfolio" program, advises U.S. investors to think of foreign investors as our creditors. "You always want to know what your creditors are thinking, especially if they ever pull the plug on you and sell." What's the chance of that occurring? Rogers says many countries hold dollars because it is politically astute, and they want to keep the U.S. Congress thinking favorably toward them. But political winds can change. Rogers practices what he preaches. He recently returned from a 22-month, 65,065-mile motorcycle trip around the world talking to foreign investors in person to determine their sentiments toward U.S. bonds and stocks. And being a capitalist, he wrote a book about his adventure entitled *"Investment Biker: On the Road with Jim Rogers."*

Monitoring overseas investors can "reduce your risk and enhance your return," agrees Larry Jeddeloh, chief investment strategist for Resource Capital Advisors, Minneapolis-based publishers of *The Institutional Strategist*. "As the world becomes more interlinked through trade, technology and communications, what happens in Frankfurt this morning can have an impact on the New York market." Jeddeloh says the key is knowing what foreign investors think of the dollar at all times. "Non-dollar investors will buy U.S. bonds based on the health of our currency. If foreigners see a weak dollar and disgorge bonds, it's an opportunity for Americans who have no investments overseas. They can buy bonds at a bargain rate and not have any currency risk at home." On the other hand, Jeddeloh believes U.S. investors should consider putting 25 percent to 30 percent of their assets in foreign bonds in countries with strong economies and currencies. This, he feels, could add 1 percent to 1.5 percent to your annual investment rate of return.

Other investment professionals say the world is vast, fast and complex; it is very difficult to track specific sentiments of foreign investors in making your own investment decisions. "You've got 2,200 hedge funds formed in the last twenty-four months that are swamping the markets with massive dollar amounts and are doing currency speculation—the deutsche mark versus the Danish kroner, yen versus the dollar," says Mike Hamilton of The Leuthold Group, a Minneapolis-based investment strategy firm. "The traditional investor should buy a professional's foreign expertise (via a mutual fund) because he or she does not have the short-term trading skills needed today to win."

Indeed, Wayne Angell, chief economist of Bear Stearns & Co. and a member of the Board of Governors of the Federal Reserve System from 1986 to 1994, contends "there isn't a great necessity to be tuned in to world developments if you're investing mainly in treasuries." Angell says "as long as the U.S. dollar remains the world's reserve currency, international rates will tend to trade off treasury rates." Still, he does think investors should monitor foreign attitudes toward the Fed. "If there is a lack of confidence in the Fed providing long-term stability for the dollar against gold and other world currencies, there could be some shift away from the dollar and that would be reflected in U.S. treasuries prices.

Angell concurs "we are in a new era of integrated world capital markets," and investors in the U.S. and abroad can "choose the currency" for holding their financial investments. Trade policies are as important as monetary policy in making that choice. Says Angell, "The dollar will always remain in an advantaged position as long as U.S. consumer and capital goods markets are always more open to investors." Foreign exporters selling in to the U.S. will want to borrow the currency from the country in which they can service the debt by selling more goods. And that bodes well for the greenback.

Another astute global observer, John Liscio, who writes *The Liscio Report* in Upper Montclair, New Jersey, says most American-based investors in government securities should pay closer attention to trade flows and a foreign country's economy than its subtle currency twitches. "The Japanese are less of a force today because they've gone from net investors to net sellers in, say, real estate, and that has put upward pressure on U.S. interest rates."

Yet W. Robert Hoye, the articulate and outspoken editor of *Quantum,* an international investment newsletter published in Vancouver, flatly maintains that bond investors looking for answers and advice around the world should first tune out the hype they hear at home. "In retrospect, the global bond market fiasco of 1992 and 1993 became a mania fostered by some very sophisticated sales pitches for bond mutual funds."

Hoye says investors new to the U.S. Government market should look for "comfort and reward." How? Buy the highest quality short-maturity treasury and, if the indicators are correct in suggesting that an upward trend in interest rates could last through 1996, roll it over at each maturity and earn a higher yield. "That way, you get preservation of capital and the magic of compound interest and you do not have to worry about what is happening in Hong Kong."

22

TAXES AND TREASURIES: IT'S NET, NOT YIELD, THAT COUNTS

For investors, there is a single truth to always remember: it's not how much you make but how much you keep that really counts.

Taxes are a fact of life, one of the two sure things in this world, and depending on where you live, they can take some voracious bites out of your gross income. We've emphasized in this book that many investors never consider the risk consequences they face in chasing the promise of high yield. The same can be said of tax consequences.

Investors in treasuries and other U.S. Government bonds, for example, enjoy some terrific tax advantages. However, few people really take the time to understand the exemptions they do and do not receive. Fundamentally, interest income earned in owning treasury bills, bonds, and notes is exempt from state and local income tax. However, that same interest is subject to federal income tax. Furthermore, any gains in the value of the treasury that are realized while you hold the instrument are subject to federal, state, and local taxes. This includes any capital appreciation you make in a treasury or government bond mutual fund.

A good rule to remember is that under current tax law, all gains or market profits realized from any stock, bond or commodity are taxed at the federal and state levels. Uncle Sam and the state and local tax collectors are not about to subsidize any part of your success in timing investment market moves. At the same time, though, state and local governments are willing to grant tax exemptions on the income you earn from investing in their debt. Consider it a "thank you" for loaning them money and an incentive to keep you reinvesting in their various securities.

However, apart from the fact that interest income from treasury bills, notes, and bonds is exempt from state and local taxes, it is impossible to make a similar blanket statement on other U.S. Government securities. "Many agency debt instruments are exempt from state and local taxes but not all are," warns CPA Chuck Rosenblatt, a tax partner with the Los Angeles accounting firm of Roth, Bookstein & Zaslow.

To make matters even more confusing, some state tax courts have overturned their previous rulings and levied taxes on income from agency bonds that, in other states, remain tax exempt.

Before you consider an investment in any government security, ask your tax professional for advice on the tax implications.

Indeed, these considerations can be daunting for government bond investors. Investors in mutual funds that hold a mix of treasury and agency bonds may find their monthly income is not state tax-free as it would be if the fund were 100 percent invested in treasuries. Many all-bond mutual funds add corporate, Ginnie Mae, or Fannie Mae bonds to their portfolios to boost yields. "You may even lose the state tax exemption on the portion of the income attributed to the treasuries," says Rosenblatt. Again, check with your tax professional or with tax officials in the state where you reside.

Generally, municipal bonds are the only debt instruments where the interest income is exempt from federal taxes. Income from munis is also exempt from state and local taxes, but usually only in the state that issues them. Subtract any fees or commissions and you get an accurate idea of what goes in your pocket.

In fact, accountants urge government bond investors to always look for the net return when evaluating investment alternatives. "Look at the yield after all taxes are paid because that's the one that counts," cautions Jack Benadon, a principal with the Los Angeles certified public accounting firm of Meyer, Benadon, Shapiro. Municipal bond investors who don't want to worry about managing and monitoring should look for a single-state muni bond fund holding only obligations issued by their state of residence in order to get the double tax-free benefits of federal and state exemption.

Although a little shopping can solve that problem, investors face a bigger shock in discovering that the interest from a municipal bond is not always tax-free and could, in fact, cost them 28 percent in taxes. "Not all muni bonds are alike," warns Benadon. "Some, like private activity municipal bonds, are subject to the Alternative Minimum Tax computation and while you think you are buying a tax-free investment, you are unwittingly not."

How do you protect yourself? Insist that your bond broker check with the issuing agency in order to determine if the interest income from the muni bond you're buying is indeed a preference item for computing the AMT.

Some municipal bonds purchased after April 1993 at a discount are subject to having their gains taxed at ordinary income rates—a maximum of 39.6 percent—rather than the capital gain rate of 28 percent. This change can sometimes give muni bonds purchased at a premium a better return than those purchased at a discount when looking at the after-tax yield.

Buying municipals for their tax benefit may not always be as wise as it seems. Depending on your tax bracket and prevailing interest rates, a partly tax-free treasury or government bond may offer a high, safe yield that delivers a better net-after-tax return. Study all advantages, shortcomings, and alternatives in an investment before you commit your money.

During the 1980s, a number of tax-advantaged investment strategies were eliminated by a spate of tax reform legislation. Today, investors should make sure an investment has a reasonable chance to return a profit, instead of acting simply as a tax shield. However, some taxwise strategies remain.

If you are having an exceptionally good year and you would like to defer income to the next year, you can buy a six-month T-bill maturing in the next calendar year. You should only consider this, though, if you are firmly convinced Congress will not raise federal income taxes within the next 12 months.

Even when you invest in instruments as creditworthy as treasuries and other U.S. Government obligations, it is particularly wise today to huddle with both your broker and your tax professional.

23

MUNICIPAL BONDS: TAX-FREE BUT NOT RISK-FREE

Municipal bonds, commonly called munis, have a glamorous mystique about them. Many investors think of them as a surefire, risk-free tax shelter for the wealthy.

No way. Munis are bonds issued by states, cities, and municipalities and have the same market risks as treasuries, plus credit risks. But no other bonds—corporate or U.S. Government—have such enticing advantages.

First, the interest you earn on a muni is free of federal income tax. Furthermore, if you buy bonds issued in the state where you live, the interest can also be free of state income tax, making them double tax-free. However, five states—Illinois, Iowa, Kansas, Oklahoma, and Wisconsin—tax some of the bonds they issue. On the other hand, treasury bond income is exempt only from state and local taxes, not federal income tax.

Second—and this is critical—municipal bonds are not risk-free. Investors in munis, unlike investors in treasuries, don't have the peace of mind in knowing the full faith and credit of the United States Government stands behind the debt. Muni bonds, like corporate bonds, can default, and you can lose your principal as well as your interest.

Third, munis are tough to track. Prices and yields for individual bonds are not quoted in newspapers and only a broker can provide a bid or ask price. And while T-bonds sell in $1,000 face value increments, muni bonds generally come in lots of $5,000.

But there are two major similarities between municipals and U.S. Governments. Muni bond prices rise when interest rates drop and fall when rates climb. In short, they react to changes in monetary policy or inflation and behave as any other bonds do. A thirty-year muni is just as volatile as a thirty-year T-bond. And, like treasuries, munis pay interest semiannually. Unlike treasuries and corporate bonds, munis are not affected by the fluctuations in the value of the dollar. Why? Foreign investors do not buy municipal bonds because there are no tax benefits for them. And, since foreign investors don't accumulate holdings in munis, they do not buy and sell large amounts, thereby disrupting the municipal market.

Specifically, though, what are municipal bonds? They are debt securities or obligations sold either by a state, to finance day-to-day governmental operations, or by a municipality—a city or township—usually to raise money for a project benefiting local residents. Unlike treasuries, you cannot buy them direct from the issuer. Individual munis are sold only through brokerage firms, banks, or as shares in a municipal bond mutual fund.

The bottom line: when you invest in a muni, you're loaning out your money to a state or city government in exchange for a promised repayment on a certain date plus a fixed rate of interest.

Maturities for munis can range from one week to thirty years, so you can use them to meet specific investment goals. Before you choose tax-free bonds over taxable bonds, though, calculate the "tax equivalent yield." This is the percentage you would earn if you were paying federal taxes on the muni bond income. The tax equivalent yield is often greater than the taxable yield on U.S. Governments or even corporate bonds. For instance, assuming you are in the 39.6 percent federal income tax bracket, you would need to purchase a treasury bond yielding 9.93 percent to equal the tax equivalent yield on a muni yielding 6 percent.

The following chart shows the combined individual federal and state tax rates, which should be considered when selecting municipal investments.

Combined effective Federal and State marginal tax rates on dividends

Marginal Federal rate

State	28%	31%	36%	39.6%
Alabama	30.59	33.38	38.05	41.42
Alaska	28.00	31.00	36.00	39.60
Arizona	32.97	35.76	40.42	43.77
Arkansas	33.04	35.83	40.48	43.83
California	35.92	38.59	43.04	46.24
Colorado	31.60	34.45	39.20	42.62
Connecticut	31.24	34.11	38.88	42.43
Delaware	33.54	36.31	40.93	44.25
District of Columbia	34.54	37.56	42.08	45.34
Florida	28.00	31.00	36.00	39.80
Georgia	32.32	35.14	39.84	43.22
Hawaii	32.32	35.14	39.84	43.22
Idaho	33.90	36.66	41.25	44.55
Illinois	30.16	33.07	37.92	41.41
Indiana	30.45	33.35	38.18	41.65
Iowa	33.17	35.75	40.09	43.24
Kansas	32.64	35.45	40.13	43.50
Kentucky	32.32	35.14	39.84	43.22
Louisiana	31.11	33.86	38.46	41.79
Maine	34.12	36.87	41.44	44.73
Maryland	32.32	35.14	39.84	43.22
Massachusetts	36.64	39.28	43.68	46.85
Michigan	31.17	34.04	38.82	42.26
Minnesota	34.12	36.87	41.44	44.73
Mississippi	31.60	34.45	39.20	42.62
Missouri	31.11	33.86	38.46	41.79
Montana	33.70	36.24	40.51	43.61
Nebraska	33.03	35.82	40.47	43.82
Nevada	28.00	31.00	36.00	39.60
New Hampshire	31.60	34.45	39.20	42.62
New Jersey	32.79	35.59	40.26	43.62
New Mexico	34.12	36.87	41.44	44.73
New York	33.67	36.43	41.04	44.36
New York City	36.88	39.51	43.89	47.05
North Carolina	33.58	36.31	40.96	44.28
North Dakota	34.22	36.71	40.92	43.96
Ohio	33.40	36.18	40.80	44.13
Oklahoma	31.63	34.33	38.87	41.16
Oregon	32.67	35.28	39.69	42.88
Pennsylvania	30.02	32.93	37.79	41.29
Rhode Island	33.15	36.42	41.77	45.53
South Carolina	33.04	35.83	40.48	43.83
South Dakota	28.00	31.00	36.00	39.60
Tennessee	32.32	35.14	39.84	43.22
Utah	31.73	34.43	38.95	42.23
Vermont	32.71	35.96	41.28	45.04
Virginia	32.14	34.97	39.68	43.07
Washington	28.00	31.00	36.00	39.60
West Virginia	32.68	35.49	40.16	43.53
Wisconsin	32.99	35.78	40.44	43.79
Wyoming	28.00	31.00	36.00	39.60

Source: *The Handbook for No-Load Fund Investors*, 1994. Compiled by Deloitte Touche.

Munis are not just a smart investment for the wealthy; they're attractive if you're in the basic 39.6 percent federal income tax bracket and want to avoid additional taxable income. But, frankly, there is an art to investing in munis, and Key 24 will explain how to master it. However, let's look at an important element of municipal bonds that is often overlooked but can affect your investment returns—commissions.

Understanding how commissions on municipal bond transactions are calculated can be confusing, explains Jim Lynch, editor and publisher of *Lynch Municipal Bond Advisory,* one of the premier newsletters covering munis. He notes that charges paid by the client for muni bond transactions are not technically commissions but markups included in the offering price (when you buy) and markdowns in the bid price (when you sell). You don't see them because they are built into the price of the muni bond, but when the transaction is completed, they are transferred to your broker as a "sales credit," another word for commission.

What is a reasonable muni bond sales credit? The National Association of Securities Dealers (NASD) sets 5 percent of the principal as a reasonable guideline for markups and markdowns in over-the-counter markets. Lynch says "most municipal bond dealers use the 5 percent rule as the maximum they can charge." (Most brokerages also have a $50 to $100 minimum to cover the cost of processing a transaction.) For newly issued muni bonds, there is no markup included in the offering price. Any profits, including sales credits or commissions paid to the broker, are paid by the issuer and not the investor. Once the newly issued munis start trading in the secondary market, brokerages are free to add the markups and markdowns.

Lynch skillfully looks at the virtually hidden commission practices on large purchases or sales of munis. Basically, the smaller the transaction, the larger the commission. "Remember, your broker spends the same amount of time selling you $100,000 worth of muni bonds as $25,000. For the broker who grosses $750 in sales credit from a 0.75 percent markup on a $100,000 offering to gross the same dollar amount on the $25,000 offering, the markup included must be 3 percent." Lynch says typically the broker or the firm makes the determination to add a higher markup on the smaller quantity, but it varies. It is hard to haggle on commissions on smaller transaction amounts, but you should shop around for the best price.

Meantime, Lynch points out several commission "truisms" muni investors should know. In volatile markets where muni bond prices are moving down, the broker will collect a heftier sales credit or commission. Conversely, when muni prices are moving up, sales credits shrink. Meanwhile, muni bonds with shorter maturities have smaller built-in sales credits than longer maturing bonds. Finally, lower quality munis will pay a fatter markup to the broker who, theoretically, has a tougher time selling them. Higher quality munis have smaller markups, again, because they are easier for the broker to sell.

24

THE ART OF INVESTING IN MUNIS

For starters, munis come in several forms. The most preferable are state "government obligation" or GO bonds. Approved by the legislature, issued and backed by a state's treasury, GOs are also redeemed by the state treasury at maturity. The other version is a "municipal revenue bond," usually issued by a city to finance a public works project. Projects may range from a new sewer system to a bridge or a domed stadium, but the bonds are repaid by the revenues collected from the citizenry. Now we're talking risk. Revenue bonds can default if the project is an operational failure and doesn't generate enough cash to make the interest payments or to pay off the bonds at maturity.

How can you protect yourself against muni bond defaults? In several ways. Munis, like corporate bonds, are rated for creditworthiness by the two main business credit rating services: Standard & Poor's and Moody's. The rating reflects the underlying strength of the issuer and its ability to redeem the bond at maturity. The safest munis are rated AAA, and anything below an A rating can be chancy. Munis with B and C ratings usually carry a little higher yield but much, much more risk; they're true junk bonds.

Never buy any municipal bond rated lower than an A and never buy a high-yield or junk muni, unless you are willing to assume the credit risk. In the past, you had as much as a two-point or greater spread between yields on junkers and high-quality munis. In recent years, it has been only three quarters of one point, so why take the risk?

Here are some other red flags. Never actively trade munis unless you want to make your broker rich and yourself poor. With munis, you should hold to maturity unless you have to liquidate. Why? The secondary market for municipals isn't as liquid as the treasury markets and you could lose 10 to 15 percent of your original investment if you liquidate when interest rates are rising.

Other red flags: Steer clear of revenue bonds issued to build and operate hospitals and nursing homes; they frequently default if the medical care facility is poorly managed. Beware when a salesperson calls and asks for an investment decision on a muni bond "immediately," as if you are going to lose out on a priceless opportunity. Not true.

Zero-coupon munis can be great tools for planning for retirement or educational needs or for readying a lump sum for balloon payment at a designated future date. But there are key points to remember and specific questions that savvy investors will bring to the table before adding zeros to their portfolio.

Zero-coupon munis are even less liquid than the general muni market since most investors buy these bonds for the purposes listed above—long-range planning—and they hold to maturity rather than actively trade them. Since zero munis have been in great demand of late, they tend to trade at lower yields (higher prices) than comparable couponed munis. And, don't forget, because of these lower yields and lack of current income stream, zero munis can be quite volatile, subject to wide swings in interest rates as well as investor sentiment.

If you want to lock in a guaranteed rate of return in your zero muni portfolio, make sure the bonds you buy are noncallable and of the best credit quality. If you buy callable bonds and your yield at the time of purchase is below that call level, you should see all sorts of red flags waving. What could happen? If rates drop and the bond is called at that higher yield (lower price), you could actually lose money. In fact, this is one of the few scenarios where investors don't make a profit in the face of falling rates.

And remember, depending on where you live, muni yields in some states do not walk in lockstep with swings in interest rates and the treasury market. For example, bonds issued in states with high tax rates, like California, New York, and Massachusetts, are traded richer (lower yield/higher price) than bonds from states with no tax, such as Texas and Nevada. Your broker should be able to help you get your hands on a copy of the "blue list" showing munis currently trading, by state, both zeros and couponed bonds.

Another tip: In bear markets for stocks, brokerages try to sell packaged municipal bond investments as "safe havens." Some are called "municipal bond unit trusts," but they often hold low-quality bonds with higher yields and heavy sales fees. Smart idea: Shop four or five brokerages for the best quote on a high-quality individual muni and shop hard. Fees, commissions, and markups vary, and the muni market is the least fairly priced of all the fixed-income markets.

There are plenty of green flags to help you make a wise buy. Look for high-yielding bonds with what are called "credit enhancements." This could be either municipal bond insurance that the issuer, not the investor, buys. Or, for the ultimate in safety, the muni is escrowed to maturity with U.S. Government securities. This protects you in two ways: First, if the municipality defaults on the bond, the government securities will continue to pass the income stream to you on a tax-free basis; second, this is as close as you come in the muni market to owning the equivalent of a tax-free government bond.

Meanwhile, here are some specific muni bond investment strategies. Consider a "laddered portfolio" of maturities: a combination of three-, five-, seven- and ten-year bonds to diversify interest rate risk and keep a steady income stream flowing. Plus, stay away from long-term munis unless the yield differential is significantly higher than that for intermediate maturities. For example, buy a thirty-year muni only if it is yielding a minimum of 1.5 percent more than seven- to ten-year munis. But above all, make sure it has an A rating or higher and that you can hold it to maturity.

How do you know when you're buying a muni bond at a bargain yield? "You have to comparison shop as if you were buying an automobile or an audio/stereo system. It's easy, though, to comparison shop for munis," says Marilyn Cohen, managing director of fixed-income for L&S Advisors in Los Angeles. "First, pick the muni that meets your criteria for your laddered portfolio—credit quality and maturity," she says. "Next, compare the yield on that muni with the comparable maturing treasury," Cohen adds. You'll find the yields and maturity in the *Wall Street Journal* or in the financial section of your daily newspaper.

Then, you do some simple math. Explains Cohen: "If your tax-free muni bond is yielding 80 percent or more of the yield of a comparable maturing taxable U.S. treasury bond, then you're getting a very good value. If your muni bond yield approaches 90 percent of the treasury bond's taxable yield, you are a very astute investor. Any comparable yield over 90 percent, sell the farm, mortgage the kids, and buy those munis." Flip side: if the muni's tax-free yield is only 75 percent of that treasury bond's taxable yield, you are getting market rate of return. "Nothing spectacular," sums up Cohen, "but nothing to sneeze at either."

25

SAVINGS BONDS: A SAFE AND SHREWD INVESTMENT

It's almost an American tradition to buy a U.S. savings bond for a newborn. After all, these bonds are the one baby gift youngsters never outgrow. They never break, never go out of style, are inexpensive and can establish solid savings habits for youngsters. For adults, savings bonds are a tax-advantaged, risk-free investment that fits every budget.

Series EE savings bonds sell at a 50 percent discount from their face value. For example, a $50 bond costs $25. Or you can buy $30,000 worth, the maximum amount in any one year, for $15,000, and you pay no commissions, fees or markups on your investment.

Savings bonds, like all treasuries, are rock-solid safe, backed by the full faith and credit of the U.S. Government. They may not pay the highest yield available in the fixed-income market, but the interest rate is adjusted periodically to make them competitive. They are easy to buy; most banks sell them and companies offer Bond-A-Month payroll deduction plans for pain-free accumulation. What's more, you don't have to watch these bonds like a hawk because there is no secondary market and, hence, no price fluctuation. Just put them in a safe place, sleep tight and forget about them until they mature. Savings bonds can be redeemed before maturity if you need the cash. I would cash in my savings bonds—and I buy the maximum allowed by law each year—only if the wolf were at the door. They should be held to maturity.

There are two forms of savings bonds. The first, as we mentioned before, are Series EE savings bonds and are an appreciation-type security. You buy them at half of their face value—say $50 for a $100 bond—and they appreciate until maturity. (Savings bonds purchased on or after March 1, 1993, mature or reach face value in 18 years or sooner.) However, even when they mature, they continue earning interest—up to 30 years from the date of issue. Then, if you choose, they may be exchanged for Series HH bonds.

Savings bonds offer great flexibility for the purchaser because they are available in a wide variety of denominations: $50, $75, $100, $200, $500, $1,000, $5,000, and $10,000. Series EE bonds issued on or after November 1, 1982, and held five years or longer, earn interest at a variable market-rate, or a guaranteed minimum, whichever is higher. The effective interest rate, set every May 1 and November 1, is 85 percent of the average market interest raid paid the prior six months on five-year treasury notes.

Savings bonds have guaranteed minimum rates giving you an investment floor—currently it's 4 percent. You can't earn less than 4 percent, but you can earn more. There is no ceiling to the yield; as T-note interest rates climb, so do savings bond rates. You can hear a recorded message giving current minimum rates and semiannual market-based rates by calling toll-free 800/4-US-BOND.

Still, pay attention when buying savings bonds. Series EE bonds bought before March 1993 accrue interest monthly but post interest only every six months (from the issue date); EE bonds bought after March 1993 accrue and post interest monthly. Timing your redemption is important; you could lose up to six months of interest if you cash in one day early. Be diligent: You want to get every dime of interest due you.

Series EE bonds have a terrific extra added attraction. While, the interest earned is free of state and local taxes, you still pay federal taxes, but you can defer them. Here is a wise tax tip: If you think you will be in a higher tax bracket when the bonds mature, you can declare the interest earned annually and pay the federal taxes at your current rate. Or you can wait until you redeem the bonds and pay the taxes. Here's a second smart tip: You can exchange your Series EE bonds for Series HH bonds and continue deferring the taxes on the income you earned on your Series EE bonds for up to twenty years.

Series HH savings bonds are a tax-wise move for income investors. They are issued only in exchange for Series E (the older version of EEs) and Series EE Bonds or Savings Notes with redemption values totaling $500 or more. When you make the exchange, you have the option of continuing to defer the taxes due on your EE income.

Series HH Savings Bonds are current income securities, and you get interest paid to you every six months (which you must declare annually for federal tax purposes). They mature in ten years and can be extended for another ten years, paying interest to you the entire time. One drawback: The interest rate is fixed for ten years, and it is the guaranteed minimum, or the floor, of the Series EE that is in effect when they were exchanged for HH bonds. At this writing, the rate is 4 percent, and you live with that rate for the first ten years. If you extend for another ten years, you get the guaranteed minimum rate in effect at that time.

When savings bonds mature, or you decide to cash out, redemption is immediate. Series EE savings bonds can be redeemed without any fees or administrative charges at most banks or savings institutions that sell them. Series HH bonds can be redeemed only at Federal Reserve Banks or their branches.

Information on savings bonds is easy to get. *The Savings Bonds Question & Answer Book* answers most questions, and it's free. Ask your local bank for a copy or write to the Federal Reserve Bank of Kansas City, P.O. Box 419440, Kansas City, Missouri 64141-6440.

26

SAVINGS BONDS: A TAX-WISE WAY TO PAY FOR COLLEGE

Once simply deemed a steady, stodgy way to save money, U.S. savings bonds now sport some additional, stylish tax advantages that directly benefit anyone wishing to put money into the most valuable investment of all—education.

Since 1990, Section 135 of the IRS code has allowed American taxpayers to buy Series EE U.S. savings bonds and exempt up to 100 percent of the interest earned—depending on their tax bracket—from their income for federal taxes. But this only applies if you redeem the bonds and use the proceeds to pay tuition and fees at colleges, universities, and qualified technical schools that same year.

Bondholders can use the money to pay for their own schooling, for their spouse, or a dependent child's education. And when you consider that earnings from savings bonds are also exempt from state and local taxes, regardless of how the proceeds are used, it makes them a terrific investment vehicle.

But there are a few restrictions. First, the federal tax exemption phases out for married taxpayers, filing jointly, who have incomes between $68,250 and $98,250, and for single taxpayers earning between $45,500 and $60,500. Second, to qualify for the interest exclusion, you must have purchased the EE bonds after January 1, 1990, be at least 24 years old, and you must designate them as "education bonds" in the year of redemption.

To get the tax writeoff, the bonds cannot be bought in a child's name or with the child as a coowner—even if they are to pay for the youngster's education. If they are intended to benefit dependent children, education bonds must be issued in either one parent's name or in the name of both parents.

Education bonds can be purchased by anyone, including grandparents, but all of the foregoing rules apply. Other caveats: room, board, and books are not qualified educational expenses and therefore are not eligible for the tax writeoff. You should also try to match the total of the bond proceeds to the actual tuition and fee costs, if possible.

Here's why: if you redeem $10,000 worth of education bonds during the year and pay qualifying education expenses of $8,000, only 80 percent of the interest income from the bonds can be exempted from your federal income tax. (When reporting the savings bond interest used for qualified education expenses, report it on IRS Form 8818.)

If your income exceeds the limits set for a tax exemption, you can still reap tax benefits using savings bonds for education. You buy the bonds in the child's name, make the youngster the owner, list his or her social security number, and give your name and number as the beneficiary—not the coowner.

How is the income from the savings bonds taxed? It depends on the age of your children and how many bonds you buy. For kids under age 14, the first $600 of income is completely tax-exempt. The next $600 of income is taxed at the child's own rate (the federal minimum is 15 percent). Investment income exceeding $1,200 a year is taxed at the parent's tax rate.

Savings bond interest accrues as unearned income. It's up to the bondowner to determine whether this income is reported annually or when the bonds are redeemed. If you choose to report the income annually, your youngster has to file only one income tax return (the first year he or she owns the bonds) called an "intent return" (IRS Form 1040EZ). This notifies the IRS that your youngster plans to claim the accrued interest annually on current and future bonds.

If the child is under 14 and you elect to recognize the income annually and pay the taxes, be aware that when it comes time to cash the bonds in, the tax will be on the last year's interest. If the youngster is over 14, the income should still be claimed annually to get the $600 exemption. Thereafter, the income is taxed at the youngster's own tax rate.

However, if you are in the 39.6 percent bracket and you are buying large amounts of savings bonds for your child who is under 14, you can defer paying the federal taxes until the bonds are cashed out, sometime after your child reaches 14, simply by electing not to accrue the income annually. You don't file an intent return. It's a smart tax-savings strategy. The entire amount of interest income earned is taxed at the child's rate once he or she is 14 or older.

27

MUTUAL FUNDS: WHERE WALL STREET CROSSES MAIN STREET

Robert Fleming had the germ of a brilliant idea when he invented the forerunner to the modern-day mutual fund in Scotland back in 1873. Round up small amounts of money from many investors, pool it in a single pot, hire an expert to monitor the investment eight hours a day and make the tough decisions on when to buy and sell, then split the profits. Or share the losses.

The philosophy of mutual fund investing hasn't changed in the last 120 years. Investors share the rewards and the risks. They have a small stake in dozens, maybe hundreds, of different investments they could never afford to buy on their own. None of their personal time and angst is spent poring over prospectuses, battling with brokers, worrying over whether they should buy, sell, or stay put.

And while fund investors will never slug a bases-loaded grand slam homer and parlay a $2 stock into a $200 a share megawinner, they won't strike out shooting for the moon at the exact moment the market plunges or when that hot stock suddenly turns cold. They float when individual investors freefall.

Mutual funds offer this same bushel basket of benefits to people investing in U.S. Government securities:

• Your money is spread across a range of maturities and yields.

- Your investments are watchdogged by a pro with the experience, expertise, research tools, and market savvy to make skillful, emotion-free, strategic buy-and-sell decisions.
- You have the security of enjoying safety in numbers, as you share any interest rate jolts with your fellow fund-holders.

Plus, there is one other king-sized advantage that investors in government bond funds have over people who invest on their own: clout. Your portfolio manager has the buying power and the connections to execute a trade at the best price and institutional commission rate—a wafer-thin $\frac{1}{256}$ of a point—instead of the one to two full percentage points you would pay as a retail customer buying and selling in small lots.

As Burt Berry, publisher and owner of *NoLoad Fund X,* a monthly mutual fund newsletter, so graphically puts it: "When you buy odd lots in treasuries from your broker, you may just have access to his inventory. It could be like buying a used car. When you go to sell it back to him, he has 100 models just like yours all driven by little old ladies. In the case of trading small lots of bonds, you may or may not get the best price available from shopping the markets."

Yet there is one drawback, too. Diversification has always been a big selling point among marketers of equity or stock-based mutual funds. If one or more of the stocks in the portfolio sink, the theory is that those price drops will be offset by price gains in other stocks, and the mutual fund, as a whole, will not be jolted by a performance laggard. But in a bond fund, whether munis, corporates, or governments, a boost in interest rates will hurt every security in the portfolio. They are all fixed-income securities, and they all fall when rates move up.

Conversely, when interest rates drop, the portfolio holdings react en masse, and the net asset value (NAV), your price-per-share, posts a gain. Another disadvantage of bond funds versus individual bonds is that there is no maturity date when you get back the face value of the bonds. Funds just keep rolling over bonds as they mature. Theoretically, then, it is possible for a fund to decline indefinitely in value so long as interest rates rise. The longer the term of the fund, the worse this problem can be.

Then there is a prevailing myth about government bond mutual funds that, if allowed to perpetuate, could hurt investors. Specifically, the myth is that government bond funds have greater liquidity than individual treasuries and that when interest rates spike and prices fall, fundholders can sell out at the net asset that day.

In truth, the secondary market for treasuries is just as liquid for individual owners as for fundholders. It's just that transaction costs are likely to be lower in a fund if you made sure it was a truly cost-efficient fund before you invested. (See Key 31.)

However, even those efficiencies can be offset by greater flexibility individual investors enjoy, depending on the circumstances. For example, if bad news erupts suddenly after market hours in the United States and interest rates leap and treasury prices fall, an investor owning treasuries can always instantly sell a position in the bond market somewhere in the world, while the mutual fund investor can call in a sell order but must wait until the U.S. bond market opens before it's executed. The fund portfolio manager rarely works around the clock, but a vigilant bond broker, monitoring client positions, does.

Despite these and other tradeoffs, government bond funds are considered, in many respects, to be the Cinderellas of the mutual fund industry. And that's unfair. Sure, mutual funds have been described as "everyman's" (and "everywoman's") investment vehicle, but the spotlight seems to always fall on stock funds.

According to Investment Company Institute, based in Washington, D.C., in 1994 there were more than 5,000 mutual funds registered with the Securities and Exchange Commission. An estimated 40 million Americans have more than $2.1 trillion invested in mutual funds. However, there are only 373 mutual funds that invest exclusively in U.S. Government bonds and fewer still that hold only treasuries.

Why? Simply put, government bond funds aren't exciting. They aren't sexy. The return figures will never grab headlines in the way that Fidelity Magellan's performance has. That stock fund has delivered a constant 19.14 percent annualized return to investors over the past ten years.

What's more, investors generally do not understand the inner workings of government bond funds. Nor do they realize that government bond funds can efficiently fill voids in their investment portfolio and, more importantly, can be used to target—and reach—specific investment goals.

28

THE FUNDAMENTALS OF GOVERNMENT BOND FUND INVESTING

A generation ago, investment lore had it that people who bought government bonds only wanted safety and income. Maybe that was true before the great and sudden popularity of the certificate of deposit. CDs are simple: Sign up and hand over your money for awhile. Today, I find investors who are in short to intermediate maturity no-load mutual funds want capital appreciation, too.

The problem is, they sometimes over-diversify in bond funds. We've all heard the mantra of spreading the risk to smooth out market fluctuations. That's wise when your pie consists of stocks, bonds, real estate, and cash. But diversifying among, say, three different intermediate U.S. Government funds because you want to pit portfolio managers against each other is a redundant exercise. All three funds will react to interest rate changes almost identically.

However, if you do have a strong sense that interest rates may decline, and want to diversify for yield, consider putting 5 to 10 percent of the investible assets and no more in a so-called junk bond fund, perhaps another 15 percent in an A- to AAA-rated corporate bond fund, 60 percent in a short- to intermediate-term government bond fund, and the remaining 5 percent in a thirty-year T-bond fund. Remember, you've introduced credit risk to a portion of your portfolio, but you're opening the door for possible higher yields.

Meanwhile, where bonds fall short is in protecting investors from inflation. Sure, you get a stream of income while bonds mature or while you remain in a bond fund, but it's no secret the dollars you walk away with when you cash out will be worth less than the dollars originally invested. To protect yourself against inflation, if you're doing retirement planning, consider putting a portion of your assets into three-month or six-month T-bills or a T-bill fund. Treasury bills track inflation very closely. In the early 1980s, when inflation soared to double-digit levels, T-bill yields kept pace.

There are dozens of very fine newsletters and advisory services to help investors select the fund that's right for them. It would be nice to subscribe to a cross section so you could mine and compare the informational nuggets. But there is also a wealth of information in mutual fund prospectuses, the SEC-inspected offering circular provided on request to investors. Here is what to look for and compare. If any information is missing, check with the fund itself or steer clear:

- Investment objective: Spells out what the fund is trying to achieve and how it invests to reach that goal. A fund, by law, cannot deviate from its stated objectives.
- Net asset value history: Shows NAV growth (or loss) on a quarterly and year-end basis.
- Income and capital gain history by quarters and totals.
- Fees, specifically management fees, loads (front and rear), 12b-1 fees, dividend reinvestment fees.
- Expense ratio: Avoid anything over 1 percent for bond funds.
- Total return: The crucial performance yardstick.
- Portfolio composition: Percentage of cash, bonds, options, derivatives, or common stock.
- Portfolio holdings: What you see is what it owns—amounts, value, maturity, percentage of net assets.
- Average weighted maturity: Gives you an idea of how rate changes will impact the portfolio as a whole.
- Portfolio manager: How long has the current manager been with the fund—in other words, is he or she the one responsible for the fund's track record, or is someone else?

29

YOUR BOND FUND GOAL: CAPITAL PRESERVATION

Before you invest, make sure the vehicle will get you to your destination, safe and sound. The fact is that government bond funds, like treasuries themselves, are not the right funds for capital growth. Do you want to build you assets and want to see big numbers? Stick with stock funds and pray you find a talented mutual fund manager.

Instead, government bond funds are designed for investors who want to preserve their capital and generate a monthly income stream. Or investors who want to park money at a yield higher than a bank pays, without freezing the funds in a certificate of deposit. Or who want tax-advantaged yields with rock-solid safety, something municipal bond funds can't deliver.

However, competition for the investor dollar is a lovely incentive to innovate, and in the last few years we've seen specialized mutual funds that give investors the same play on bad news as well as many of the same sophisticated strategies that they can get from buying individual governments in the secondary market. A new crop of bond funds allows you target maturities just as if you were buying the treasury itself. Others deliver the same highly leveraged advantages of zeros or stripped coupon treasuries without having to pay hefty commissions.

In short, U.S. Government bond funds today can replicate all of the same advantages of buying individual U.S. Government securities, while eliminating many of the shortcomings. But you must know how to buy them, what to look for, and what to avoid. That's right. Not all bond funds are created, structured, and managed equally. They have a bewildering number of different fees, features, investment objectives, performance histories, and total returns. Just as treasury investing is a lot more complicated than it appears to the average buy-and-hold-to-maturity person, you must shop government bond funds diligently until you find one that matches your personality, risk tolerance, and financial objectives—one that fits like a glove.

The big question, though, before you set off on a shopping trip is whether the time-honored concept of mutual funds really is right for you. Unfortunately, there are no easy answers. It boils down to asking yourself some highly personal questions that really dictate the direction you take as a treasury investor.

First, if you want convenience and you don't mind paying for it, a carefully selected no-load U.S. Government bond fund makes sense. The fund's portfolio managers watch the Fed for you, monitor the market-moving news out of Washington and world financial capitals for you, negotiate with brokers and dealers for the best price and execution, and fashion sophisticated yield-enhancing strategies on your behalf.

Second, if you have only a limited amount of money to commit to the fixed-income component of your investment portfolio, you may find that a mutual fund is a wise choice. After all, one treasury bill would cost you $10,000.

Third, if you agonize, freeze, or procrastinate when it comes to making hard buy and sell investment decisions, mutual funds are for you. Portfolio managers are professional decision-makers. Individual investors in treasuries may find themselves in contrarian positions watching friends fleeing with the pack at a time when the market is signalling a buy.

There is peer pressure in investing, but if you read the market accurately and don't try to fight it, you'll find it's invariably right.

However, the mutual fund approach to treasury investing might not be right if you have a firm conviction on interest rates and you want to pursue it at every end of the market—short, long, and intermediate. Or if you want the ability and flexibility to try sophisticated strategies like leverage, puts and calls, and futures—in short, if you want to get involved with the market and call your own shots on your own terms. If you want hands-on involvement, team up with a seasoned bond broker and forge a client relationship based on mutual trust and respect.

If you feel more comfortable in a mutual fund, let's go shopping with the pros and find the right one.

30

CHOOSING A GOVERNMENT BOND FUND: ASK THE HARD QUESTIONS

With 373 open-end government bond funds—60 of which are invested exclusively in treasuries, 34 closed-end government bond funds, 154 U.S. Treasury money market funds, and another 183 money market funds investing in U.S. agency debt obligations—picking a solid, steady performer that meets your financial goals is no cakewalk.

The mutual fund industry has discovered the investor marketplace is a bare-knuckle, free-for-all where investors must be sold, not just informed. The results: cold-calling brokers, screaming full-page ads, direct mail blitzes, and siren-song seminars that all but guarantee big profits and promise financial security forever.

Indeed, with more than 5,000 mutual funds selling their expertise, it isn't surprising that the investor is barraged with seductive statistics and enticing claims. But government bond funds are a breed apart. True, the fundamentals are the same, but bond funds have peculiarities of their own, like modest returns, so their virtues often get lost in the scramble for towering yields.

Let's start with the age-old argument of load versus no-load mutual funds. So-called "load" mutual funds are usually sold by investment brokerages; the load, of course, is a commission shared by the firm, the salesperson, and sometimes a separate selling organization or wholesaler known as the sponsor. The traditional loads have been dropping, though. Government bond funds charge anywhere from 3 to 5 percent—and the rate could decline depending on how much you invest. Still, it is cash creamed off the top—so you start off in the hole. If you pay the maximum load, your government bond fund must post a 5 percent return just to recoup your commission and get you out of the red.

The archrival of the load fund is the no-load fund. No-loads started as no-frills alternatives to load funds and have quickly captured investor fancy. Most of the cash invested, in theory (but not always in practice) goes into the portfolio. Investors sign up for no-load funds by clipping and mailing a coupon or calling an 800 number. Some of the biggest names in the mutual fund world such as Dreyfus, Fidelity and Vanguard dropped their loads in the early 1970s when a stock market plunge sent investors scrambling for the safety of banks and other depository investments. But loads and other fees are coming back in fashion.

Lately, a hybrid has emerged—the low-load fund. Fidelity Investments, the largest of the mutual fund families, has added low-load funds with the sales commission around 3 percent for stock funds. Low-load U.S. Government bond funds typically charge less than 3 percent—anywhere from 1.5 percent to 2.25 percent—and, again, it's right off the top. Some fundwatchers are outraged that former no-load funds are collecting any load at all, feeling there is no justification for it. With no sales force to compensate, the commission is going straight into management's coffers.

Do load funds outperform no-load funds? "The presence or absence of a load has nothing to do with fund performance," reports Burt Berry, publisher of the widely-respected *No-Load Fund X* newsletter, based in San Francisco. He cites a *Wall Street Journal* inquiry into this very question—the investment performance of no-load funds was found to have a "slight edge" over load funds.

Nevertheless, any load, regardless of size, is a prohibitive expense for anyone investing in U.S. Government bond funds. A spectacular return in a government bond fund currently is about 8 to 9 percent annually depending on maturities. By comparison, a stock mutual fund with a hot-handed portfolio manager in a strong year could produce double-digit returns of 15 to 20 percent or more. Stock fund investors reaping that kind of reward might not grumble over paying a one-time 3 to 5 percent sales commission. But anyone investing in a government bond fund will never see huge double-digit returns unless we have another 1980s bull market in bonds with a dramatic drop in interest rates. Hence, investors should think twice about paying any load. It's a direct drain on total return—the key performance measurement that includes net asset value increases plus capital gains and dividends.

Not all loads are levied up front. Not long ago, some mutual funds imposed what they called a "deferred sales charge." It penalized investors, on a sliding scale, for cashing out of the fund. The first-year charge was 5 percent, second-year was 4 percent and so on, disappearing in the sixth year. Meantime, these same funds, by not charging a front-end sales commission, promoted themselves as no-load or "NL" funds. Fortunately, for investors, the Securities and Exchange Commission cracked down on the practice and forced them to fully disclose and explain the nature of the fees. Nowadays, this is called a "redemption fee." Again, this is a totally unnecessary cost, nothing more than a hind-end load, and any U.S. Government bond fund charging one should be avoided.

Far more common, less expensive, but a rip-off nonetheless, is an expense the Investment Company Institute, the mutual fund industry trade organization, lobbied past the SEC about a decade ago. It's called rule 12b-1, and it allows mutual funds to charge fund investors a fee to cover advertising, marketing, and promotional expenses. The SEC failed to put a ceiling on the fee, but the idea quickly caught on and about half of all mutual funds impose one; the amount ranges from .25 percent to 1.25 percent each year that the investor remains in the fund. View any 12b-1 charge as a red flag and avoid any funds that levy it.

Yet another hidden fee to watch for is a commission for reinvesting dividends into the fund. One of the prime advantages of investing in a mutual fund is the automatic reinvestment feature; you don't have to remember to do it yourself. Dividend reinvestment fees were a customary practice in the 1960s. Some fund managers even charged a fee or commission for investing capital gains, an egregious act if there ever was one.

Still, there are other hard questions to ask. Few investors, for example, ask if U.S. Government bond funds are guaranteed in any way by the government. Reg Green, who heads *Mutual Fund News Service,* says, "The U.S. Government only guarantees to pay a specific coupon rate of interest semiannually and repay the principal when the bonds mature. The government does not guarantee to protect you against market risk." Green's advice: Play detective and ask every question you can think of about the safety of your money before you invest.

31

FINANCIAL DERIVATIVES CAN BEDEVIL FUND INVESTORS

Mutual fund investors may have a new problem, and it may take some sleuthing to uncover it. Some portfolio managers of U.S. Government bond funds and money market mutual funds are using what are called "financial derivatives" to boost yields and, in several instances, the strategy is backfiring.

Derivatives have been blamed for the first failure of a money market mutual fund in 16 years. In September 1994, Community Bankers U.S. Government Money Market Mutual Fund collapsed when its sponsor, Community Assets Management of Denver, Colorado, could not raise enough money to cover losses in the portfolio. As a result, investors were expecting to lose 6 cents of every dollar they had in this money fund. The real shock is that money market mutual funds, while not government guaranteed, have earned a reputation as a safe, solid place to park cash.

What happened? The money market fund's portfolio manager, Prospect Hill Advisers of Milwaukee, Wisconsin, invested $35.5 million of the fund's $84 million assets in a financial derivative of a government bond called "structured notes." These are debt instruments where the interest rate and/or the principal are often indexed to an unrelated indicator such as short-term interest rates in Japan. Structured notes can also have a floating interest rate tied to a foreign currency like the German deutsche mark. The problem is that they are

106

usually private transactions made by the fund portfolio manger and are not liquid. So when the Federal Reserve Board began raising short-term interest rates in early 1994, Prospect Hill Advisers could not sell off or liquidate the structured notes in its portfolio, and fund investors faced a huge loss on their money.

The use of financial derivatives in mutual fund portfolios is hardly new or sinister. Until recently, though, derivatives have been known only to portfolio managers and sophisticated institutional investors; private investors had no reason to worry about them. For instance, portfolio managers would take positions in short treasury futures to shorten the duration in a bond fund portfolio. This hedging strategy would make it less sensitive to interest rate fluctuations.

A Planned Amortization Class Collateralized Mortgage Obligation, another financial derivative, would give portfolio managers a clear picture of how the cash would flow from Fannie Mae and Freddie Mac bonds in a U.S. Government bond fund.

However, in the early 1990s, when interest rates were trending downward and bond prices were soaring, "A variety of derivatives were used defensively not only to hedge interest rate risk, but to pump up performance," says Jeff Kelley, associate editor of *Morningstar Mutual Funds.* "But liquidity is the real concern. These derivatives contracts are often exotic, customized transactions between two parties. They do not trade daily, and it is very hard to determine what they are actually worth until you go into the marketplace and try to sell them. If the portfolio manager is forced to sell in an unfavorable market, he could experience substantial losses and so can the investor." When interest rates started climbing, portfolio managers holding derivatives tied to rate-sensitive indicators were further squeezed.

Morningstar, which watchdogs and rates mutual fund performance, says traditional U.S. Government bond funds continue using derivatives to enhance performance, especially bond funds that invest in government mortgage securities like Fannie Mae and Ginnie Mae securities. However, investors often do not take a close look at the fund prospectus to see if the portfolio manager is buying—or has the right to buy—interest only or "IO" notes or principal only or "PO" notes. These are very speculative derivative investments structured from mortgage bonds that react differently to interest rate movements. IO notes fall in value when interest rates fall because people refinance their mortgages and eliminate some future interest payments. PO notes rise in value when rates fall because people get their principal back sooner than they expect.

"Even an investor who really scours shareholder reports will find it very hard to determine what the amount of derivatives or the amount of volatility the fund could experience because of derivative exposure," says Kelley. And his colleague, Catherine Voss-Sanders, also an associate editor adds: "There are quite a few lawsuits [being filed] about lack of adequate disclosure. If it doesn't look like the fund is invested in traditional government bonds, call up the mutual fund manager and ask."

What are the tipoffs? Look at the shareholder report. If the description of the bond is lengthy but not really meaningful to a lay person, there may be some exotic derivatives in the portfolio. "Some good clues are a series of numbers and letters after the bond description," suggests Jennifer Newport, a *Morningstar* analyst. Terms in the prospectus like deutsche mark linked, IO, PO, IFRN (Inverse Floating Rate Notes) are also red flags. "This doesn't tell you how risky the mutual fund actually is, but it should alert you to ask the fund manager how much of the portfolio is (or can be) invested in these kind of derivatives. You should also ask yourself, 'Do I understand the potential risk here?'"

Just how widespread is the problem of mutual funds troubled by exotic financial derivatives? Between 1993 and 1994, four of the nation's largest banks and brokerage firms had to inject more than a half billion dollars into their own government bond mutual funds to offset derivative losses.

Ironically, mutual fund industry specialists say the derivative issue is overblown. The Investment Company Institute, the trade association representing the mutual fund industry, candidly discusses the issue, and explains that traditional investment vehicles like options, forward contracts, futures, and interest rate swaps are all used as financial derivatives along with the aforementioned structured notes. Reg Green, head of *Mutual Fund News Service* in Bodega Bay, California, says, "Most mutual funds do not use derivatives because they are too risky. But you have to check out the prospectus to be sure."

The bottom line message to investors in mutual funds: Do not try to become an expert in financial derivatives. But do take the time to explore whether your fund is investing in them. It could save you considerable grief.

32

WATCHING FUND EXPENSES

Ferreting out hidden costs and bypassing U.S. Government bond mutual funds that bristle with a variety of charges is absolutely essential. The lower the fees, the greater the return—and that, of course, is especially important in a bond fund where returns are generally lower than stock funds.

Are there benchmarks? Look for a total expense ratio today of about 1 percent or less and avoid bond funds that exceed it. This is a combination of management, investment advisory, custodial, and legal fees, plus transfer fees and distribution fees divided by the average assets outstanding. The largest component of this is the annual management fee, which should average around .40, or less than one half of 1 percent of your total investment. The management fee pays for the portfolio manager's time and talent and covers the fund's administrative costs and overhead. The good news? Total expenses on bond funds are trending downward; four years ago the expense ratio benchmark was 1.25 percent and management fees averaged .50 percent.

"Expense ratios and sales charges are much, much more important in bond funds than stock funds," stresses John Rekenthaler, editor of *Morningstar Mutual Funds,* which closely tracks the internal operations and performance of over 5,000 mutual funds, including almost every government bond and treasury fund. Rekenthaler contends that bond portfolio managers are not entitled to a richer management fee than .40 percent "because the amount of value the manager can add to your return by making correct decisions is much less than in a common stock fund. The range of returns is narrower."

To illustrate, *Morningstar* says the best performing all-treasury bond fund for 1993 returned 31.57 percent to investors, while the worst performer in the group produced a 2.27 percent annual return. "But, remember, these are volatile long-term treasury bond funds, and interest rates were declining," he says. (In 1994, with interest rates on the rise, long-term treasury bond funds were not delivering this kind of return.) "By comparison, equity (stock) fund returns were all over the planet in 1993," says Rekenthaler. "Some standouts returned more than 40 percent. Some lost money—9 percent." Meanwhile, expense ratios for government bond funds in 1993 ranged from a whopping 2.85 percent for the EV Classic Government Obligations Fund to .05 percent for Franklin's Institutional Adjustable Government portfolio.

In a new trend, designed to attract investors, about ten government bond funds, such as United Services Intermediate Treasury Fund, charge no expenses at all. Many times management will absorb costs to attract new capital when a fund is just starting out. If you are an investor lured by yields, you should know a fund can stop absorbing expenses at any time—when they do start charging you, it comes straight out of the yield. Sure, zero expense is a come-on—but if you check out the fund (is it backed by a strong mutual fund family, and is the portfolio manager a veteran?)—it could benefit total return.

Once you've identified a list of government bond funds with an acceptable expense ratio, whittle the group down to a few that meet your investment goals and have a good track record with high average yield. Some purists might argue that this is attacking the problem from the wrong direction. The key to performance here is ridding the investment vehicle of excess baggage and then finding a fund that fits.

Locating the right mutual fund starts with the prospectus. By federal law, all mutual funds are investment companies and must file a prospectus with the SEC. The prospectus contains the Investment Objective and what the fund invests in to reach that goal. For example, Dreyfus Short-Intermediate Government fund, a no-load mutual fund that has earned a very rare five-star rating and buy recommendations from *Morningstar Mutual Funds,* says it seeks "current income." Translated, its fund manager is looking for maximum yield with low risk. For the twelve months ended September 1994, it yielded 7.04 percent by investing "mostly in treasury notes and some government obligations," says Rekenthaler. While this is not a sky-high yield, the editor says, the Dreyfus fund earned *Morningstar*'s coveted five-star rating "because it is hard to see any weaknesses here. Excellent returns, competitive yields, low expenses and a great cost structure."

Now, here is a prime example of where it pays to do your homework. According to its prospectus, Dreyfus Short-Intermediate Government fund has no load or sales commission, no redemption fee when you liquidate, and a 0.40 percent total expense ratio that includes the annual management fee. That means the majority of your capital goes straight into the portfolio and goes to work for you. Indeed, less than a half-percent is a small price to pay for five-star rated performance where the minimum investment is only $2,500.

33

BOND FUNDS: FINDING THE BEST DEAL

Investors are too often the new victims of the old shell game. They see a whopping yield in some promotional brochure or ad and visualize the money in their pocket, never asking for proof or the names of other investors.

Mutual fund investors have had their share of disappointments—and hard dollar losses. Enticed by big performance numbers, they are convinced history can repeat itself. You see it mainly in stock funds. The mythical Interplanetary Fund had a 21 percent average rate of return over the last ten years. However, take a close look at Interplanetary and you discover the fund posted big double-digit returns only in its early years. After the portfolio manager was hired away by a competitor, the fund performed miserably for the past few years. To get the big picture, look at each piece.

That is true for U.S. Government bond funds. Investors often chase the highest yield to boost monthly income. Fund managers know this and sometimes take risks, adding longer maturities to the portfolio even though it deviates from the portfolio policy. Here are some tricks of the trade that have bilked unfortunate investors who believed all U.S. Government bond funds are rock-solid and risk-free.

For example, an intermediate seven-year treasury note may be yielding 7.30 percent, but an intermediate government bond fund portfolio manager needs an edge—a higher yield—to attract new investors and generate new management fees. So he may spice up the fund with other debt instruments that could be riskier and, hence, pay a higher interest rate. Warns Paul A. Merriman, portfolio manager for the five Merriman Mutual Funds in Seattle: "If you look carefully at the prospectus, the fund might have a right to hold 15 to 25 percent of other debt. They could be lower-graded, higher yielding investments, foreign government bonds, or zero-coupon bonds that wouldn't pump up current yield but would add more volatility than investors expect." More recently, so-called derivatives—the more volatile elements on higher-yielding mortgage bonds, have been found in government bond funds. But investors and the press have quickly caught on to the danger of derivatives and other "exotics" as yield-hyping strategies with steep downsides.

"People stand in line to get these yields but they don't understand the risk," explains Gerald W. Perritt, editor of *The Mutual Fund Letter,* a Chicago-based newsletter. "The shock for investors comes later when the notes and bonds in the portfolio start maturing and are redeemed at par—$100. To protect yourself, Perritt advises you ask the fund salesperson or customer service representative for an estimate of the fund's "total return," not just "current yield." Then ask if the portfolio manager sticks with the fund's objectives as stated in the prospectus or does he have the freedom to experiment to pump up the yield. If you don't get a straight, clear answer, stay away.

Perritt, one of the more vocal watchdogs of the mutual fund industry, has another gripe. "One of my big complaints is, when you see a list of government bond funds, the connotation is that you are buying a fund that invests in U.S. treasuries. But what you end up getting is a fund nearly 100 percent invested in Ginnie Maes, and they can be treacherous." These, of course, are government agency bonds issued—and backed—by the Government National Mortgage Association, not by the U.S. Treasury. They pay a yield two to three points higher than treasuries because they often have maturities as long as the 30-year T-bond and are as volatile as that T-bond, too. When interest rates climb, Ginnie Mae bond prices drop sharply and bond fund investors lose principal.

But here's the rub. When rates drop, homeowners tend to refinance their houses and the underlying mortgages are often paid off or called, frequently at no profit to the holder. For investors lured into the fund by the rich yield, it's a little like heads, you lose; tails, you lose or break even.

Nevertheless, other mutual fund managers will write (sell) call options on bonds held in their portfolios to pump up yields and, hence, monthly income. This is a side contract giving an outside investor the right to purchase the bond at a certain price within a specific time in exchange for a cash payment called a premium. The portfolio manager writing the option bets interest rates won't move beyond a certain range. Thus the option won't be exercised, will expire worthless, and the fund keeps the premium as a capital gain.

However, even though the option-writing practice is fully disclosed in the fund prospectus and investment objectives, there is some risk to fundholders. If interest rates do drop and the bond price rises to what's called a striking price, the option holder can call the bond away, and the mutual fund investor doesn't participate in the profit. And if interest rates rise, call option writing doesn't protect the fundholder from more than a modest price loss, so the net asset value tumbles. (See Key 19 for more on options.)

"Investors are getting wary of all the call options written on government bond funds," says John Rekenthaler, editor of *Morningstar Mutual Funds*. "In theory, short-term gains are distributed to shareholders along with any other income received by the fund to boost the apparent yield." He feels this practice, although legal, is risky deception at best. "Technically, short-term capital gains are not a true component of yield, while call options are very damaging to a mutual fund's long-term total return," contends Rekenthaler.

34

BOND FUNDS: FREE CANAPÉS AND COSTLY LUNCHES

If some U.S. Government bond mutual fund managers resort to risky ploys to raise yields and win new investors, other managers pare their expense ratios to beef up the all-important profit barometer—total return. How? As mentioned, new-to-the-market mutual funds will waive the management fee as a promotional ploy to lower expenses and bring in dollars. But here's the catch: once the portfolio is plump with dollars, the management fee inevitably appears.

Mutual fund marketing experts know from experience that investors will rarely bail out unless horrendous performance or a disastrous market eats deeply into capital, and holders flee for survival. Caveat: The canapés are often free but the lunch isn't. Obviously, these strategies are designed to build up the fund as quickly as possible. Plus, as indicated, a waived management fee is just that— waived temporarily. It's likely to reappear, so expect it. In the meantime, keep your eye on the fund's bottom line— your total return.

Conventional wisdom in mutual funds holds that it's wise to join a fund family like Kemper, Fidelity, or Vanguard so you can re-allocate your assets easily and quickly with a telephone call. In theory, that's a brilliant concept. Just make sure you are not charged a switching fee for moving money.

Few people actually change funds within a family unless, again, the market has taken a sudden turn for the worse. The trick here is to do your homework and make sure sister and brother funds within the family have a

116

good track record, because you do not want to switch out of a tainted darling into a dog.

Many of the biggest mutual fund families like Fidelity have some of the better performing funds because they can afford top talent, and they know they can ill afford to have just one or two superstar funds to bring investors in the front door. They frequently offer several different variations on the government bond theme—all treasuries. They may be a combination of treasuries and Ginnie and Fannie Maes, or highly targeted funds that invest in zero coupon bonds.

Even if you think you are too busy or too inexperienced to pick a U.S. Government bond mutual fund or if you feel uncomfortable reading red and green flags that may be waving, there are options. For instance, there are money management firms that invest their clients' assets in no-load mutual funds, instead of individual stocks or bonds. These specialized firms monitor the performance of several thousand different mutual fund portfolio managers. When market conditions change or a fund's performance drops off, these firms may move the clients' assets from one mutual fund, or fund family, to another.

You do not pay a fee to switch between mutual funds; however, you do pay a fee for this advice and certain specialized services. These services may include setting investment goals, determining risk tolerance, and fund selection, according to Kurt Brouwer, president of Brouwer & Janachowski, a San Francisco investment advisory firm that uses only no-load funds to manage money. The fee: usually 0.50 to 1.50 percent, depending on the size of your account.

Finally, always look for an edge that will save you time, mistakes, and anxiety. If you like to take charge of your own money but still want a fixed-income professional actually making the buy and sell decisions— Charles Schwab & Company, the nationwide discount brokerage firm, offers its Mutual Fund Marketplace. With a single toll-free phone call, this gives you access to more than 850 no-load and low-load stock and bond mutual funds. Fidelity Investments also has a Funds

Network that sells 350 no-load mutual funds beside the funds in Fidelity's own family. Other discount brokerages offer similar services.

In fact, you can really be creative with your investment strategies and be safe at the same time. Say you own a $25,000 bond with coupon interest of $1,200 a year. You really don't want to sell the bond, but you seem to dribble away the semiannual income. Or at the very least, you aren't getting the benefit of compounded interest. A smart strategy is to keep the bond and endorse over the interest checks to an astutely managed money market fund investing in U.S. treasuries.

35

KEEPING AN OPEN MIND ABOUT CLOSED-END FUNDS

A mutual fund, by definition, usually is an open-end investment company. It continually sells and redeems shares, and you own shares of the net assets. Again, that is the total market value of an investment company's shares—securities, cash, and any accrued earnings—minus its liabilities, and divided by the number of shares outstanding.

A mutual fund can also be a closed-end investment company. It issues a fixed number of shares, and they are traded in the securities or stock market. They're usually bought and sold through stockbrokers. There are about 34 closed-end bond funds with primarily treasury and government agency obligations in their portfolios. Some invest in foreign government obligations.

Closed-end bond funds offer the investor an edge. They pay dividends and often sell at a discount to their net asset value (NAV) (although they can sell at a premium). You should rarely buy a closed-end bond fund at its initial public offering because it is usually priced at 100 cents on the dollar or higher, perhaps 106. Several months later, it almost always sells at a discount of 5 to 10 percent of its net asset value.

Thomas J. Herzfeld, probably the savviest of all closed-end mutual fund investors and author of the *Encyclopedia of Closed-End Funds,* has a strategy of buying only the most deeply discounted funds and watching interest rates and stock market behavior. "You have to see which way the market is moving in government bonds and the direction of share prices for closed-end funds," says Herzfeld. That takes skill because the closed-end bond fund's share price in the stock market is not tied to the net asset value of the portfolio.

Hence, you can be right on an interest rate call and the portfolio's assets will expand, and wrong in the stock market because, for some unfathomable reason, the fund's per-share price can drop. Still, the wider the discount between the stock price and the NAV, the greater your potential for gain—especially in a closed-end U.S. Government bond fund.

Here, in the mid-1990s, Herzfeld says there are great bargains in closed-end U.S. Government bond funds. Theoretically, he says, you can be buying the most solid treasury and agency obligations for as little as 85 cents on the dollar. And it's not that rare to find closed-end fund shares trading 15 percent off the net asset value. What's more, it looks very promising for investors. "Regardless of which way interest rates go from here," adds Herzfeld, "I have not seen so many wide discounts to net asset values since the 1981 low in the bond market."

Tagline: Closed-end fund investors are always looking for Judgment Day. That's the day closed-end funds go open-end and the discount immediately disappears, ensuring an automatic gain. The fact is, closed-ends don't open that often. But when they do, it's a windfall.

35

THE DOWNSIDE OF MUNI BOND FUNDS

Municipal bond mutual funds also have their short-comings. Fund investors give up the fixed rate of interest they reap with an individual muni bond. The yield, while paid out as monthly dividend income, is an average of all munis in the portfolio.

"You really have to look at 'total return' and not just 'yield,' in evaluating a muni bond fund," stresses Sheldon Jacobs, editor and publisher of *The No-Load Fund Investor.* "You want dividends (income distribution) and capital appreciation. And like all government bond funds where returns rarely match stock fund returns, look for the highest performers with the lowest expenses."

Jim Lynch, editor of the *Lynch Municipal Bond Advisory* newsletter, points to a second shortcoming. "Investors should be aware there is no maturity date in a municipal bond fund. This point is frequently glossed over. Technically, with a muni bond fund, there is no assurance of a payback of principal like there is with an individual municipal bond." Adds Lynch: "The risk in buying a bond fund is that you must sell to get your principal back and you are subject to the vagaries of the muni bond market. If you had bought in to a bond fund at the end of 1993 and sold in September 1994, you would have principal loss." With the individual muni bond you can hold it to maturity; however, if you need to liquidate, you can sell—but you face market risk.

A third shortcoming can be the mix of the bonds in the portfolio. In choosing a muni bond fund, read the prospectus to make sure the high tax-free yield isn't the result of overloading the fund with municipal revenue bonds that are issued by cities to finance public works projects. Since these bonds are repaid by revenues collected from the citizenry, they can default if the project is poorly run and doesn't generate enough cash. Obviously, these would carry higher risk, so the more generous payout could come with strings attached.

A fourth factor is that, if you're in a high tax bracket, some municipals in a bond fund can trigger the Alternative Minimum Tax, which will actually add to your tax bill, notes Jacobs. The AMT, as it's called, may be triggered if you have enough tax preference deductions such as oil depletion allowance and accelerated depreciation as well as interest from a type of muni called a "private activity bond" issued after August 7, 1986.

How do you know if a fund portfolio holds bonds that will affect your AMT? You can use the fund's toll-free number to call the portfolio manager and hope you get a straight answer. But there's always that worry because of bond turnover in the portfolio. Otherwise, you should consider a muni "unit trust" where the bonds do not change. Best advice here is to consult your tax professional.

The fifth thing to avoid is funds where the portfolio is stuffed with thirty-year munis. Generally, with a flat or inverted yield curve, you do not get that much more income by going 15 to 30 years out compared to a portfolio comprised largely of intermediate maturities—seven to ten years. If you do have a positively sloped yield curve (see Key 12), and when the thirty-year is yielding 1.5 percent more than ten-year maturities, it may be worth going into those longer bonds. But plan on staying in for a while rather than jumping out at the first jolt. And remember, a thirty-year muni is every bit as volatile as a thirty-year T-bond, so be watchful if the fund you're considering holds only long-term municipal bonds. These bonds will subject the fund to greater interest rate volatility and sharper swings in value.

The sixth red flag occurs when interest rates are on the rise. When bond prices are falling, many municipal bond funds will be forced to cut their dividend. This flag was really waving in 1994 when the Federal Reserve increased interest rates several times and muni bond prices eroded. Dividends shriveled. This is a double whammy for investors who bought into muni bond funds for the tax-free income stream only to have it dwindle. On top of that, they lost principal. This is a compelling argument for buying individual municipals in a laddered portfolio as discussed in Key 24.

Before you invest, research the performance and risk records of tax-exempt bond funds in references like the thirteenth edition of the American Association of Individual Investor's *Guide to Low-Load Mutual Funds.* This publication ranked Vanguard's Intermediate Term Muni Fund as its top performing tax-exempt muni bond mutual fund from 1990 through 1994 with an 8.2 percent total annual return and a "below average" risk ranking.

That proves you can have it both ways—top performance and low risk. And if your muni bond fund is part of a family offering free exchanges, you can always switch into cash if you see an extended storm on the horizon.

In the meantime, if you can find a double tax-free mutual fund, where the portfolio holds only munis issued in the state where you reside, you could be home free, tax-free that is, and not pay a penny of taxes on the monthly income.

How difficult are they to find? Any of the mutual fund information resources cited in this book—*Morningstar,* American Association of Independent Investors or the annual mutual fund issues of *Money Magazine, Kiplinger's Personal Finance, Forbes, Barron's, Worth, Smart Money, Business Week*—list them. Indeed all but eight states have single-state mutual funds buying their municipal bonds. (Alaska, Delaware, Illinois, Montana, Nevada, Oklahoma, South Dakota, and Wyoming do not.) New York City residents may get the best deal of all. A New York City tax-free muni bond gives investors income that is exempt from federal, state, *and* city income taxes, making it a triple winner. It's not a painkiller for high-bracket taxpayers, but it can certainly help.

37

HARD TRUTHS AND SMART STRATEGIES FOR INFORMED INVESTORS

No matter where you put your money to work, remember this wisdom and adopt it as a fundamental belief: the informed investor who has skills to win has a better chance of being successful than the misinformed investor who needs luck to win.

Nowhere is this a harder truth than in the U.S. Government securities markets. The world of treasury bills, bonds, and notes and their fixed-income siblings—agencies and munis—can no longer be categorized as simply "the bond market" where all investments act the same. Different sectors of the bond market perform independently, which is a new phenomenon.

For instance, we learned in the Persian Gulf crisis of 1990 that short-term interest rates fell because the market anticipated that the Federal Reserve would ease monetary policy to avoid recession, while long-term interest rates rose because the threat to the world oil supply triggered inflationary fears. Conventional wisdom always told us that all interest rates move in the same direction—but no longer.

These new phenomena demand that you explore hard truths and analyze time- and-market-tested strategies for informed investors.

The first, most fundamental step for investing in U.S. Government securities is to make a decision about interest rates. Will they go up? Will they go down? Will they stay put? What is the general trend?

If you've done your homework, read the periodicals and listened to the gurus, and you are still genuinely unsure, stay short-term. Buy three-month, six-month, or one-year T-bills and roll them over. You have liquidity, a yield comparable to money market mutual funds, and a temporary floor if rates go down.

However, when you do form an opinion on interest rates—whether bullish (rates will drop, bond prices will rise) or bearish (rates will climb, prices will fall)—you must then pick a maturity sector. The farther out you go on the maturity spectrum, the greater the price volatility, hence the higher the risk and the larger the reward. As we've said before, short and intermediate maturities (one to seven years) will react less dramatically, in terms of price fluctuations, than longer maturities—T-bonds with ten- to thirty-year maturities.

After forming your opinion on rates—and feeling comfortable with them—your next strategic step is to set a stop loss. Informed investors are disciplined, know how much they can lose and when to admit they are wrong.

Of course, that's easy to say (or write) but very tough to practice. Humans, by nature, hate to admit they're wrong. They rationalize, blame, freeze—do anything but admit they've made the wrong decision. For investors, that can be financially fatal. And in the long bond market, where, if you're long, even the slightest interest rate move against you can send prices—and your principal—plunging, not admitting you've made a mistake can be a very costly lesson in arrogance or ignorance.

So, form an opinion on rates, pick a maturity and set your stop losses.

Now, don't assume I've taken a header over the edge when I state, "You'll make more money when you're wrong than when you're right." To this, I must add, "if you're disciplined."

Let's go back to human nature for a moment. Most investors not only can't admit they're wrong, but they can't help committing the cardinal sin—they think the market is wrong and they're right. So, they do the worst thing possible—they add to a losing proposition—and then they lose even more as the market continues to drop. If they're investing on leverage, they get a margin call for more cash. And when the pain becomes unbearable, human nature dictates that the investor sell out and vow never again to go back into the market.

What should you do when you've made a wrong decision? Admit it as soon as possible, sell out, and reverse your position; if you were bearish, lock in a bullish position or vice versa. It's a slap to your pride, ego, and finances to confess that you made a mistake. We all hate failures. But if you act fast enough, you can capitalize on the error while other investors either become paralyzed by their losses or sour on the market.

Let's take another seemingly illogical step. The best thing that can happen to you, believe it or not, is to lose money in your first forays into the treasury market. If you win right off the bat, you can become cocky and emotional and throw discipline out the window. Instead of setting up stop losses on every position, you feel you have the Midas touch.

What's more, you tend to reward yourself on early victories by selling out and crowing. It may be difficult for a loser to admit defeat, but it's just as hard for winners to enjoy their success by letting the winnings run and adding more positions. The axiom to cut losses and stick with winners is another hard truth that really applies to the fast-moving treasury market.

Losing cleanses the soul. When you're in a losing trade, you can't think straight until you make that disciplined decision to cut the losses and the pain and reverse your position. Your investing is a business, and business owners discontinue or discount merchandise that doesn't move; they don't sit on it or bail out of the business. They hold a clearance sale and restock.

The same is true for investors. If you are going to do more than just hold to maturity and clip coupons, you must learn to be a professional loser before you can ever become a professional winner.

QUESTIONS AND ANSWERS

Q. I'm a physician with a pension plan, and I'm not planning to retire for another ten years. Most of the assets are in a money market fund, but some of my colleagues told me I should be in zero-coupon treasuries. What's the smartest strategy?

A. Without knowing your personal financial situation, goals, and needs, it is impossible to make a firm recommendation one way or the other. But, here are some "pro" and "con" guidelines. On the plus side, zeros allow you to pick your maturities and lock in a fixed rate of appreciation. Zero treasuries are safe and secure.

On the negative side, if interest rates go up, you are locked in at a lower yield to maturity, and zero-coupon bonds will depreciate faster than a comparable maturing treasury paying interest. Why? Because the coupon has been stripped off, there is no income to reinvest at higher rates. Nevertheless, if you see higher rates on your horizon, a sounder, simpler strategy might be to invest in three-month treasury bills and roll them over when they mature. Then you can take advantage of higher yields, should that occur.

Zero-coupon treasuries are most beneficial when interest rates are declining because you are locked into a high rate of return, and the bonds will rapidly appreciate.

Q. I understand the Treasury issues a special class of savings bond that is tax-free if the proceeds are used to pay for a child's college education. How does that work?

A. This is true, but it's not limited to children or college. Section 135 of the IRS Code says taxpayers can buy U.S.

savings bonds to educate themselves, their spouse or their children and get up to 100 percent exclusion on their income tax. These are called "education bonds" and may also be used to pay costs for a qualified trade school or technical training program.

But there are some catches. The tax exclusion is designed to benefit people who really need it. It phases out for married taxpayers earning between $68,250 and $98,250 and for single taxpayers with incomes between $45,500 and $60,500, adjusted for inflation. Plus, to get the full exclusion, educational bonds cannot be purchased in the child's name; they must be bought in the name of the taxpayer.

On balance, if you qualify, savings bonds are a great way to build a tax-advantaged nest egg to pay for schooling. You can start small—a $50 bond costs only $25 in cash today—or buy as much as $30,000 in one year for a cash outlay of $15,000. And even if you don't use them for school, Series EE bonds have an array of nifty features. (See Keys 25 and 26)

Q. What is the most cost-effective way to buy Treasury bills?

A. Direct from Uncle Sam. You can buy T-bills from most banks and brokerage firms, but chances are you'll be charged a $25 to $60 administrative fee or commission, depending on whether it's a newly auctioned bill or one trading on the secondary market. However, all branches of the Federal Reserve or an office of the Bureau of Public Debt will sell you one at no cost.

Buying from the government is remarkably simple. You can buy newly auctioned treasuries through the mail by submitting a noncompetitive tender, thus automatically opening a TREASURY DIRECT account. You receive your own account number for subsequent purchases and eliminate the middleman.

When you buy direct, though, all purchases must be accompanied by full payment—cashier's check, certified personal check, maturing treasury securities, or cash. Forget cash, though. You don't want to walk around with or mail the minimum $10,000 that a T-bill costs.

Contact your local Federal Reserve Bank or branch or write to Bureau of Public Debt, Department N, Washington, D.C. 20239-1500.

Q. I've been thinking of investing in government bond funds and was told to look into both open-end and closed-end funds. What's the difference between them?

A. An open-end fund is what most investors think of when you mention mutual funds. This type of fund creates new shares on demand as investors deposit money for purchases. Shares are bought at the net asset value and can be redeemed at any time for the prevailing market price, which can be higher or lower than the original purchase price. Open-end funds can be invested in stocks, bonds, money market instruments, or a combination of these, depending on the objectives of the fund, and can be classified as no-load (0 percent commission), low-load (under 3 percent commission) or high-load (5 percent commission). Research has shown no correlation between superior performance and high loads; I always recommend no-load funds so that all your money goes to work for you and is not siphoned off to pay a salesperson's commission. Closed-end funds issue a fixed number of shares and usually are bought and sold on a major exchange. These funds normally trade at a discount to their net asset value and do not continually issue new shares to meet the demand of deposits by investors. Closed-end funds, like stocks, with a set number of shares issued and tradable, respond more closely to the law of supply and demand and the desires of the marketplace than do open-end funds.

Q. I'm aware that T-bills, notes, and bonds have no credit risk since they are backed by the full faith and credit of the U.S. Government. What about government agency securities like Fannie Mae and Sallie Mae bonds?

A. The dozen or so agencies in the U.S. Government such as the Federal National Mortgage Association (Fannie Mae) or Student Loan Marketing Corp. (Sallie Mae) issue obligations backed by Uncle Sam, and the federal government, so far, has not allowed any agency to default on its debts (bond issues). However, these agencies do not carry the "full faith and credit" guarantee that makes them completely worry-free. In the past, agencies generally paid higher coupon rates to encourage investors to consider them instead of credit risk-free T-bills or T-bonds as a parking place for their cash. But agencies aren't the great deal they used to be, because the yields they generate are not that much higher than those from intermediate to long-term treasuries. And there is less liquidity in the agency market, with wider spreads between the bids and asks on these bonds. A final point to consider is that the income from some agencies is not exempt from state and local taxes; after paying these taxes on a higher coupon agency bond, you can end up netting less than if you had placed your money in a lower coupon T-bond. Be sure and check with your tax professional before committing your cash to buy an agency. And if you're looking at fund expenses, government bond funds that include agencies in their portfolios to raise their yields often charge a higher management fee than funds invested in all treasuries.

Q. I have $10,000 of "risk" money that I want to invest. Is this enough to put into the treasuries market and be able to reap significant rewards?

A. You might want to consider putting the multiplying power of leverage to work for you by buying or selling puts and calls on treasury futures. This is a very active and liquid market, but it is not for the conservative or novice investor; options on treasury futures are a form of gambling, and you need to have the knowledge and the stomach for it. And you must have a definite opinion about interest rates and their direction before you place your "bet." Buying calls reflects your thinking that bond prices will rise (interest rates will drop) before the expiration date on that option, and buying puts means you are convinced that bond prices will drop (as interest rates rise). Although there are no guarantees protecting your principal, if you bet wrong on interest rates, you are not hurt as badly with options on futures as with buying the treasury future itself. You can choose not to exercise your option to buy the contract at its expiration date, thereby losing only the premium you put up initially to own that option. (Premiums can range form a few sixty-fourths up to $5,000 plus a flat commission fee for the transaction.) There is no ceiling on what you can "win." But remember, most investors lose money in the options market, so just like a casino, the odds are against your "beating the house."

Q. I am considering putting some of my money into a government bond fund. My broker tells me just to pick the one with the highest yield. Is it really that simple?

A. With government bond funds, it's tempting to look for the highest yield in order to increase monthly income. But remember, higher rewards are usually generated by exposing yourself to greater market risk. Not all government bond funds are rock solid and risk free. Read the prospectus for any fund you are considering to see if management stretches the parameters of fund policy to create the illusion of higher yields. Do they add longer maturities that suffer from larger price fluctuations and expose shareholders to greater market risk? Does the portfolio show a recent infusion of premium bonds with high coupons that generate high current yield but will actually dole out a loss when the bonds redeem at par? Make sure you ask for estimated "total return" to weed out these false expectations. Look for government agency bonds that may be boosting yields. Ginnie Maes, for instance, pay high yields because of their long maturities—which also means they're extremely volatile. Also, because these bonds are actually clusters of home mortgages, when interest rates drop and homeowners refinance, the Ginnie Maes are called and paid off, frequently at no profit to the holder. If the prospectus mentions option-writing as part of the investment strategy, watch out for more "heads you lose, tails you lose or break even" scenarios. These can generate short-term gains that are not technically a true component of yield and can be damaging to long-term total return. Also, check the prospectus to see if the portfolio manager uses exotic financial derivatives to boost performance. Clues: Bonds followed by a series of numbers and letters; terms like IO/PO notes, IFRN, or references like "linked" to a foreign currency or overseas interest rates. Bottom line: Be a smart shopper.

Q. I used to buy U.S. Government T-bonds, have them registered in my name and delivered to me. I recently made another purchase, and now my broker says I can't have them delivered to me. He says they've changed the system, and I shouldn't worry. What's going on? What happens if my brokerage goes under and I don't have a certificate to cash in at the Treasury?

A. Your broker is referring to what is known as "book-entry" system. At the time of purchase, book-entry securities that are not represented by a certificate are registered in your name on the books of the U.S. Treasury. Many new issues of bonds fit this format because it cuts down on paperwork on the brokerage level and saves the investor from worry about lost or stolen certificates. You do not need to be concerned if your brokerage goes out of business since these bonds are guaranteed by the full faith and credit of the U.S. Government. The Treasury knows you as the owner of the bonds because of the entry made on its books; additional proof you should plan on submitting at the time of redeeming the bonds would include the confirmation you received at the time of the purchase and a copy of your monthly statement from the brokerage showing positions held in your account.

Q. I study the financial pages of my newspaper every day for the prices given on treasury bonds and bills. Then, when I call my broker before the market opens to see about making a purchase, the quote he gives me is usually not the same as the one in the paper. Why is that?

A. The quotes you see in the financial pages are representative of prices paid on transactions of $1 million at the close of trading, or as close to 4 P.M. Eastern Time as possible, the prior business day. But remember, U.S. treasuries trade almost around the clock, around the world. So, by the time you're reading your morning paper and before trading even begins in New York, Chicago, or Los Angeles, Japan has transacted a full day of business and traders in London have been buying and selling for half their day. This activity by U.S. investors doing business with foreign brokers or by foreigners purchasing U.S. securities abroad sets the tone for the opening prices for buyers and sellers stateside.

Q. I'm confused about commissions when buying or selling treasuries through my broker. What should I expect to pay?

A. Two watchwords are in effect here: "ask" and "negotiate." There is no set schedule of commissions charged by all brokers on treasury transactions, so you need to ask the hard questions up front to determine how much of a bite potential brokers will be taking out of your investment dollar. They should not shy from walking you through the numbers of a transaction, step by step. If you're told that there is no commission on a particular trade, especially when dealing with new issues, be wary, and turn the tables. Ask what price you would be able to receive if you chose to sell that same security; the difference between that and the purchase price is the commission or markup the firm is factoring into the transaction. You should be no less careful when discussing mutual funds; ask what the load is on a fund that the broker recommends. Remember, loads are commissions paid by the fund to a broker or salesperson; the broker who is truly watching out for your best interests will recommend a no-load fund that meets your investment goals and does not merely generate commissions. And if you don't like what you hear, negotiate. You and your broker should be able to reach a compromise that is fair to both of you. If you show you are savvy, you can operate from a position of strength in building a foundation for a candid and profitable relationship.

GLOSSARY

Accreted Interest   The difference between the price of a bond bought at an original discount and its face value; generally, the increased value is pro-rated over its life and recognized annually as ordinary income. Example: zero-coupon bonds.

Accrued interest   Interest earned but not yet received on a bond between semiannual coupon dates. The buyer of the security pays the quoted dollar price plus accrued interest, and the seller receives the interest earned to date at the time of sale.

Arbitrage   The art or, as sometimes is believed, the science by which one buys certain securities thought to be undervalued and simultaneously sells other overvalued securities. Most frequently used in government securities with yield curve transactions. Example: buying two-year T-notes and selling thirty-year T-bonds in a belief the yield curve will steepen to a more positive slope (see Key 12).

Ask   The price at which a security is offered by a seller.

Back up   (1) When yields rise and prices fall, the market is said to back up. (2) When investors swap out of one security into another of shorter current maturity. Example: out of a five-year note into a two-year note.

Basis point   One one-hundredth of 1 percent (0.01 percent).

Bearer bond   A bond that is not registered in the name of the owner and requires clipping of semiannual coupons in order for the paying agent or issuer to disburse the interest. Whoever presents the coupons receives that interest payment. More common is the book-entry registered bond where the owner receives semiannual interest through automatic electronic transfer from the issuer. (The Treasury has not issued bearer bonds since 1982, and only 250,000 remain outstanding.)

Bid   The price a buyer is willing to pay for a security.

Bond indenture   A formal agreement between a bond issuer and bondholder giving specifics of the bond, including issuer requirements and redemption rights.

Book-entry securities   The Treasury and most federal agencies have moved to a book-entry system where securities are not represented by engraved pieces of paper but are maintained in computerized records at the Fed under the names of member banks, which in turn, keep records of the securities they own as well as those they are holding for customers. Since 1986, all new Treasury securities issued are in this form.

Broker   A person who brings buyers and sellers together for a commission paid by the initiator of the transaction or by both sides; a broker does not take a position.

Call   An option that gives the holder the right but not the obligation to buy the underlying security at a specified price during a fixed time period.

Callable   Redeemable by the issuer before the scheduled maturity. (When interest rates significantly fall, bond issuers can save money by floating a new issue at a lower interest rate.) Call features are spelled out in detail, either in a bond indenture or a prospectus.

Capital gain   The sale price of a security minus the purchase price.

Carry   The interest cost of financing securities held.

Commission   A broker's fee for handling transactions for a client.

Competitive bids   Tenders submitted at auctions by dealers (and others) when buying securities. The Treasury selects the highest and lowest acceptable yields, and the dealers/buyers within that range "win" the bid. (See **noncompetitive bid.**)

Coupon   (1) The annual rate of interest on a bond's face value that a bond's issuer promises to pay the bondholder. (2) A certificate attached to a bearer bond evidencing interest due on a payment date.

Credit risk   The risk that a borrower will be unable to make payment of interest or principal on time.

Current yield   A bond's coupon divided by its price.

Dealer   In contrast to a broker, a person who acts as a principal in all transactions, buying and selling for his or her own account.

Derivative   Instrument that gets its value from another security; its rate of return is based on the underlying security's performance.

Discount bond   A bond selling below its redemption value and generally paying interest below the current coupon rate.

Dutch auction   Single price auction; dealers submit bids, and the market clearing price—highest accepted yield—is the price all buyers (competitive and noncompetitive) receive.

Exercise price   The price at which an option holder may buy or sell an underlying security; also called the striking price.

Expiration date   The deadline when the holder of an option must exercise this option.

Federal funds   Funds deposited by commercial banks at Federal Reserve Banks, including funds in excess of bank reserve requirements; can be lent to other member banks on an overnight basis at the Federal Funds Rate.

Federal funds rate   The rate of interest at which Fed funds are traded. This rate is generally pegged by the Federal Reserve through open-market operations.

Federal Reserve Board (FRB)   A federal agency empowered by Congress to regulate credit in the United States. Its members are appointed by the president.

Federal Reserve requirements   The percentage of its deposits that a commercial bank must set aside, determined by the Federal Reserve, in order to limit its potential credit-granting capability. The current requirement is 10 percent.

Federal Reserve System   A system of Federal Reserve Banks in the United States forming twelve districts under the control of the Federal Reserve Board. These banks regulate the extension of credit as well as other banking activities.

Financial planner   A professional who evaluates and counsels individuals and corporations on their financial status and goals. Their compensation may be fee only, commissions, or a combination.

Forex market   Foreign exchange market.

Form 1099-OID   An IRS form listing taxable interest on zero-coupon securities or treasury bills. Required to be mailed to some holders of zeros.

Futures market   A market in which contracts for future delivery of a commodity or a security are bought and sold.

Governments   Negotiable U.S. Treasury securities.

Handle   The whole dollar price of a bid or offer. For example, if a security is quoted 98–16 bid and 98–17 offered, 98 is the handle. In quoting the market, traders would generally omit the handle and refer only to the spread 16–17, which represents 16 to 17 32nds.

Inflation   A general rise in prices.

Interest-only "IO"   IO mortgage-backed securities represent the interest from a pool of mortgages. IO investors suffer when homeowners pay off their mortgages early by refinancing because they lose the chance to collect years of interest.

Inverse floater   A floating-rate note whose interest rate increases as market rates decline.

Leverage   A strategy that offers the possibility of high return for a small cash outlay by requiring only partial payment for the security and financing the remainder of the purchase price.

Liquidity   An asset that can be converted easily and rapidly into cash without a substantial loss of value. In the money market, a security is said to be liquid if the spread between bid and ask prices is narrow.

Load   Difference between the net asset value and the price at which a mutual fund will sell shares. This is usually the commission paid to a broker or salesperson for selling the fund.

Long bond   U.S. Treasury security with a long maturity. Currently, the government issues long bonds with an original maturity of thirty years.

Margin   The purchasing of securities, either stocks or bonds, on leverage. Generally, though, the interest rate charged for margining a security is higher than the repurchase or repo rate for leveraging bonds.

Market value   The price at which a security is trading and could presumably be purchased or sold.

Maturity (date)   The date on which a bond comes due; both principal and any accrued interest due are paid on this date.

Mortgage-backed security   A collection of mortgages bundled into a single security and then sold to private or institutional investors as such.

Municipals   Securities issued by state and local governments and their agencies.

Net asset value   The actual value of a bond fund that charges no load.

Noncallable   Cannot be redeemed at the option of the issuer. Most treasuries are noncallable securities.

Noncompetitive bid   The price you agree to accept—it is the average yield of the accepted competitive bids on Treasury securities at auctions and the method most people use when purchasing bills, notes, or bonds through TREASURY DIRECT.

Odd lot   Less than a round lot.

Off-the-run issue   In treasuries and agencies, an issue that is not included in dealer or broker runs. With bills and notes, normally only current issues are quoted.

On-the-run issue   The most actively traded issues, usually those that were most recently auctioned.

Premium bond   A bond selling above par or face value.

Primary dealer   Any of the firms (currently thirty-nine) recognized by the Federal Reserve Bank who bid regularly on the Treasury's offerings.

Principal-only "PO"   PO mortgage-backed securities represent the principal from a pool of mortgages. PO notes rise in value when rates fall because people get their principal back sooner than they expect.

Put   An option that gives the holder the right but not the obligation to sell the underlying security at a specific price during a fixed time period.

Repurchase agreement (RP or Repo)   An agreement between a holder of securities and an investor to repurchase securities at a fixed price on a fixed date. The security buyer in effect lends the seller money for the period of the agreement, and the terms of the agreement are structured to compensate the buyer for this. Dealers use RPs extensively to finance their positions. Exception: When the Fed is said to be doing RPs, it is lending money—that is, increasing bank reserves.

Reverse repurchase agreement   Most typically, a repurchase agreement initiated by the lender of funds. Reserves are used by dealers to borrow securities they have shorted. Exception: When the Fed is said to be doing reverses, it is borrowing money—that is, absorbing reserves.

Round lot   In the money market, round lot refers to the minimum amount for which dealers' quotes are good. This is usually $1 million in notes and bonds and $5 million in bills.

Savings bonds   Bonds issued through the U.S. Government (Series EE at a 50 percent discount from face value and Series HH in exchange for $500 or more of EE bonds) in denominations from $50 to $10,000. The interest is exempt from state and local taxes. If elected, no federal tax comes due until the Series EE bond is redeemed; HH bond interest must be reported each year.

Secondary market   The market in which securities are traded after initial auction.

Settlement date   The date on which a trade is cleared by delivery of securities against funds. Normally, government securities are settled on the next business day.

Short sale   The sale of securities not owned by the seller in the expectation that the price of these securities will fall or as part of an arbitrage. A short sale must eventually be covered by a purchase of the securities sold.

Spread   The difference between the bid and the asked price in the secondary market.

Structured note   A bond that also includes one or more derivative contracts bundled up to give a return tailored to the view of a particular investor or category of investors. Derivatives can be piled one on top of the other within a structured note so that the gain (or loss) on the note will far exceed any change in the value of the underlying asset. This is called a leveraged note.

Trade date   The date on which a transaction is initiated. The settlement date may be the trade date or a later date.

Treasury bill   A treasury obligation issued in minimums of $10,000, with $1,000 increments, up to $1 million with maturity dates of three months to one year. It is issued at a discount from face value (which determines the interest rate and investment yield).

Treasury bond   A treasury obligation issued in minimums of $1,000, with $1,000 increments, up to $5 million for maturities of 10 to 30 years, carrying a fixed interest rate and issued, quoted, and traded as a percentage of its face value.

TREASURY DIRECT   System for individuals to purchase treasury securities at auctions directly from the Federal Reserve Bank with no fees or commissions. Securities are held in book-entry form and interest is paid electronically to a specified checking account.

Treasury note   A treasury obligation issued in minimums of $1,000, with $1,000 increments, up to $5 million for maturities of one to ten years, carrying a fixed rate of interest. Exception: The minimum denomination for two- and three-year notes is $5,000.

Volatility   The characteristic of a security, commodity or market to rise or fall sharply within a short-term period.

Yield curve   A chart or graph showing the relationship at a given point in time between the current yields of short-term, medium-term and long-term bonds that expose the investor to the same credit risk. The most common yield curve is for treasury securities.

Yield to maturity   The rate of return yielded by a debt security held to maturity when both interest payments and the investor's capital gain or loss on the security are taken into account.

Zero-coupon bonds   Bonds that make no semiannual interest payments and are sold at a deep discount from face value, and interest is accreted. Created when a brokerage strips the coupons off a T-bond and sells the corpus (principal) separately from the coupons. Examples of government zeros are CATS, STRIPS, and TIGRS.

APPENDIX

THE FEDERAL RESERVE
AND ITS BRANCHES

In addition to the office of the Board of Governors of the Federal Reserve System in Washington, D.C., there are twelve main branches of the Fed and twenty-two local offices. Each one has a Public Affairs Office that can supply investors with a wealth of free pamphlets, charts, statistics, special publications, and audiovisual materials about the Fed system, monetary policy, financial markets, and the economy. Their addresses and phone numbers are listed below.

Board of Governors of the Federal Reserve System
Publications Services
MS-127
Washington, DC 20551
(202) 452-3244

Federal Reserve Bank of Atlanta
Public Affairs Department
104 Marietta Street, NW
Atlanta, GA 30303-2713
(404) 521-8788

Birmingham Branch	(205) 731-8500
Jacksonville Branch	(904) 632-1000
Miami Branch	(305) 591-2065
Nashville Branch	(615) 251-7100
New Orleans Branch	(504) 593-3200

Federal Reserve Bank of Boston
Public & Community Affairs
P. O. Box 2076
Boston, MA 02106-2076
(617) 973-3459

Federal Reserve Bank of Chicago
Public Information Center
230 South LaSalle Street
P. O. Box 834
Chicago, IL 60690-0834
(312) 322-5111

    Detroit Branch   (313) 961-6880

Federal Reserve Bank of Cleveland
Corporate Communications & Community Affairs
Department
P. O. Box 6387
Cleveland, OH 44101-1387
(216) 579-3079

    Cincinnati Branch   (513) 721-4787
    Pittsburgh Branch   (412) 261-7800

Federal Reserve Bank of Dallas
Public Affairs Department
2200 North Pearl Street
Dallas, TX 75201-2272
(214) 922-5254

Federal Reserve Bank of Kansas City
Public Affairs Department
925 Grand Avenue
Kansas City, MO 64198
(816) 881-2402

    Denver Branch   (303) 572-2300
    Oklahoma City Branch   (405) 270-8400
    Omaha Branch   (402) 221-5500

Federal Reserve Bank of Minneapolis
Public Affairs
P. O. Box 291
Minneapolis, MN 55480-0291
(612) 340-2446

Helena Branch   (406) 447-3800

Federal Reserve Bank of New York
Public Information Department
33 Liberty Street
New York, NY 10045
(212) 720-6134

Buffalo Branch   (716) 849-5000

Federal Reserve Bank of Philadelphia
Public Information (for typical consumer inquiries)
P. O. Box 66
Philadelphia, PA 19105-0066
(215) 574-6115

Federal Reserve Bank of Philadelphia
Research (for economic and business outlook)
100 North Sixth Street
Philadelphia, PA 19106

Federal Reserve Bank of Richmond
Public Affairs Department
P. O. Box 27622
Richmond, VA 23261
(804) 697-8109

Baltimore Branch   (410) 576-3300
Charlotte Branch   (704) 358-2100

Federal Reserve Bank of St. Louis
Public Information Office
P. O. Box 442
St. Louis, MO 63166
(314) 444-8808

Little Rock Branch	(501) 324-8272
Louisville Branch	(502) 568-9200
Memphis Branch	(901) 523-7171

Federal Reserve Bank of San Francisco
Public Information Department
P. O. Box 7702
San Francisco, CA 94120
(415) 974-2163

Los Angeles Branch	(213) 683-2903
Portland Branch	(503) 221-5900
Salt Lake City Branch	(801) 322-7926
Seattle Branch	(206) 343-3638

BROADCAST RESOURCES

The following television and radio business programs as well as cassette tape services provide news, analysis, and opinion on the U.S. Government bond market plus domestic and world economic events affecting interest rate movement.

Television

ABC
    Good Morning America   with Tyler Mathison, editor of *Money Magazine* (Wednesday)

CNBC
    Today's Business   with Mark Haines & Susie Gharib (Mon - Fri)
    The Money Wheel   (Mon - Fri)

Including: How to Succeed in Business (Monday); Home Office Computing (Tuesday); Managing Your Money (Wednesday); The Real Estate Report (Thursday); The Business of Living (Friday); MoneyTalk (Monday through Friday);

View From the Top (Monday through Thursday);
Business Travel Tips (Friday); Street Talk
(Monday through Friday)

Additional Money Wheel Segments (Mon - Fri)
Wall Street Report; Newsmakers; Winners and
Losers; Futures Report; Credit Market Report;
Market Insider; The Dorfman Report; Buy, Sell,
Hold; Your Portfolio; Tech Talk. Most segments
are aired or updated several times each day.

Inside Opinion	with Ron Isana (Mon - Fri)
Market Wrap	with Bill Seidman and Bill Wolman of *Business Week* (Mon - Fri)
Business Insiders	with Neil Cavuto, Roy Blumberg, Kathleen Hays, and Bill Wolman (Mon - Fri)
Business Tonight	with Sue Herera and Dean Shepherd (Mon - Fri)
Mutual Fund Investor	Bill Griffeth (daily) joined by Jim Rogers on Friday. (Mon - Fri)
Money Tonight	with Sue Herera and Janice Lieberman (Mon - Fri)
Strictly Business	with Bill Griffeth (Weekends)
Weekly Business	with Dean Shepherd (Weekends)
Technology Edge	with Bruce Francis (Saturday)
Fortune Week	with Walter Kiechel, *Fortune's* managing editor (Weekends)
How to Succeed in Business	with Mark Haines (Weekends)

Cable News Network (CNN)

Business Morning	with Stuart Varney and Deborah Marchini (Mon - Fri)
Business Day	with Stuart Varney and Deborah Marchini (Mon - Fri)
Moneyline	with Lou Dobbs (Mon - Fri)
Your Money	with Stuart Varney (Saturday)
Moneyweek	with Lou Dobbs (Weekends)
Managing	with Lou Dobbs (Weekends)
Pinnacle	with Beverly Schuck (Sunday)
Inside Business	with Deborah Marchini (Sunday)

Public Broadcasting System (PBS)

Wall Street Week	with Louis Rukeyser (Friday)
Nightly Business Report	with Paul Kangas (Mon - Fri)
Wall Street Week in Review	(Friday)
Adam Smith (aka Money World)	(Weekly)
Bloomberg Business News	with Kathleen Campion (Mon - Fri)

Bloomberg Direct

This is a 24-hour news channel, generally broadcast through Satellite Direct TV; however, it's also being picked up by local cable stations, and some consumer news stations. Started in June 1994.

Syndicated Broadcast Programs (as opposed to cable)

Wall Street Journal Report	by Dow-Jones (Weekly)
It's Your Business	by U.S. Chamber of Commerce (Weekly)

This Morning's Business   by Viacom (Mon - Fri)

Radio

ABC Radio Network (3,400 affiliates)
Business Updates	with Gary Nunn
(once daily)	(Mon - Fri)
Money Talk	with Bob Brinker
	(Weekends)

AP Network News (750 affiliates)
Business Updates
(twice an hour × 24 hours) (Mon - Fri)

Public Radio International (500 affiliates)
Marketplace	with David Brancaccio
	(Mon - Fri)
Sound Money	with Bob Potter (Weekly)

Business Radio Network (100 affiliates)
Business Day	with Jack Lott and Kerry
(4 hours/day)	O'Brien (Mon - Fri)
Market Wrap	with Bill Bresnan
	(Mon - Fri)
Bill Bresnan Show	(Mon - Fri)
Sound Money Investor's Hour	with Ed Taxin (Mon - Fri)
Financial Power Hour	with Steve Bonnenberger
	(Saturday)
Inside Wall Street	with Mark Leibovit
	(Weekends)
All About Futures	with Moeez Ansari
	(Weekends)
Superstocks	with Jerry Wenger
	(Sunday)
Scams Across America	with Dan Rector
	(Sunday)
On the Floor	with Maxim Husler and
	Gary R'Nell (Sunday)

CBS Radio Network (500 affiliates)
    In the Marketplace   with Ed Crane (Mon - Fri)

CNBC Business Radio (80 affiliates)
    Business Updates   (Daily)
    (twice an hour × 24 hrs)

CNN Radio Network (650 affiliates)
    Business Reports   (Daily)
    (40 min. past each hour)

Wall Street Journal Radio (155 affiliates)
    The Wall Street Journal   (Mon - Fri)
    Report (hourly)
    The International Report   (Mon - Fri)
    (4 times in A.M.)
    Stock Market Final   (Mon - Fri)
    (twice after close)
    Weekend Focus   (Weekends)
    The Enterprising Manager (Weekends)
    Barron's on Investment
    (3 one-min. stories)   (Weekends)

Westwood One Radio Network (133 affiliates)
    You and Your Money   with Eric Schurenberg of
                             Money Magazine
                             (Mon - Fri)

Westwood One Entertainment (375 affiliates)
    The Bruce Williams Show (Mon - Fri)
    (3 hours)

Sheridan Broadcasting Network (214 affiliates)
    Money Smarts   with Tene Croom
                             (Mon - Fri)

Sun Radio Network (150 affiliates)
    Financial Advisor   with Charles DeRose
                             (Weekends)

Michael Martin on   (Sunday)
Real Estate

UPI Radio Network (100 affiliates)
   Business Updates   (Mon - Fri)
   (once hourly)

USA Radio Network (1,118 affiliates)
   Business Updates   (Mon - Fri)
   (once hourly)
   Consumer Advocate   with Jim Paris, CFP
                             (Mon - Fri)
   Tax Rescue Minute   with Dan Pilla (Mon - Fri)
   Money Magazine   with Jordan Goodman of
                             Money Magazine
                             (Monday)

WOR Network Radio (110 affiliates)
   Smart Money   with Ken and Daria
                             Dolan (Mon - Fri)

Audiotape & Financial News

Investor's Hotline   with Joe Bradley
(800) 345-8112
News Tracks for Executives
(609) 232-4634

NEWSLETTERS

Although lengthy, the following is only a partial list of the sources of information available by subscription or membership. Newsletters are listed alphabetically, and we have made no attempt to rank them.

I suggest you write to the newsletter publisher's office and request a sample copy. If you happen to run across an outstanding source of information for the debt market investor that is not included in this list, drop me a note, and I'll add that newsletter to the next edition of this book.

AAII Journal
American Association of
   Individual Investors
625 North Michigan
   Avenue, Suite 1900
Chicago, IL 60611

Bond Fund Advisor
IBC/Donoghue, Inc.
P. O. Box 9104
290 Eliot Street
Ashland, MA 01721-9104

Bond Market Semiotics
P. O. Box 1457
Castleton, VT 05735

Bond Market Strategy
2100 River Edge Parkway,
   Suite 750
Atlanta, GA 30328

Bond Week
488 Madison Avenue, 14th
   Floor
New York, NY 10022

*Bostian Economic
   Research and
   Investment*
26 Broadway, Suite 247
New York, NY 10004

*Bridgewater Daily
   Observations*
372 Danbury Road
Wilton, CT 06897

Bullish Consensus
P. O. Box 90490

1111 South Arroyo
   Parkway, Suite 410
Pasadena, CA 91109-0490

Bullish Review
14600 Blaine Avenue East
Rosemount, MN 55068

CNBC Insight
CNBC
P. O. Box 259
Springwater, NY 14560

*Commodity and Currency
   Comments*
BCE Place Galleria
181 Bay Street, Suite 250
P. O. Box 866
Toronto, Ontario
CANADA M5J 2T3

*Commodity Traders
   Consumer Report*
1731 Howe Avenue, Suite
   149
Sacramento, CA 95825

Early Economic Outlook
Center for International
   Business Cycle
   Research
Columbia University
475 Riverside Drive, Suite
   834
New York, NY 10115

Economics Illustrated
Bank of America
Investment Research
   Group

300 South Grand Avenue,
Suite 2500
Los Angeles, CA 90071

The Fed Tracker
4805 Courageous Lane
Carlsbad, CA 92008

FullerMoney
Chart Analysis, Ltd.
7 Swallow Street
London, W1R 7HD
ENGLAND

*Grant's Interest Rate
Observer*
30 Wall Street
New York, NY 10005

Griggs & Santow Report
75 Wall Street
New York, NY 10005

*High Frequency
Economics*
584 Broadway,
Suite 1001
New York, NY 10012

Hulbert Financial Digest
316 Commerce Street
Alexandria, VA 22314

Income Fund Outlook
and *Income and Safety*
The Institute of
Econometric Research
3471 North Federal
Highway
Fort Lauderdale, FL 33306

Industry Forecast
Jerome Levy Economics
Institute
P. O. Box 26
Chappaqua, NY 10514

Interest Rate Forecast
1002 Sherbrook Street
West, Suite 1600
Montreal, Quebec
CANADA H3A 3L6

Institutional Strategist
Resource Capital
Advisors
900 Second Avenue South
International Centre,
Suite 300
Minneapolis, MN 55402

*Investment Timing
Consultants*
31800 Northwestern
Highway, Suite 202
Farmington Hills, MI
48334-1664

*Investor's Guide to Closed-
End Funds*
Thomas J. Herzfeld
Advisors, Inc.
P. O. Box 161465
Miami, FL 33116

Jerry Favors Analysis
8382 Gilmerton Court
Dublin, OH 43017

Liscio Report
19 Belle Grove Drive
Upper Montclair, NJ
    07043

*MBH Weekly Commodity
    Letter*
Box 353
Winnetka, IL 60093

Mamis Letter
Hancock Institutional
    Equity Services
One World Trade Center
200 Liberty Street
New York, NY 10281

Market Commentary
Arbor Trading Group
1000 Hart Road,
    Suite 260
Barrington, IL 60010

*Market Trim Tabs and
    Mutual Fund Trim Tabs*
520 Mendocino Avenue,
    Suite 330
Santa Rosa, CA 95401

Money-Forecast Letter
Financial Research
    Center, Inc.
7 October Hill Road
Holliston, MA 01746

MONEYLETTER
IBC/Donoghue, Inc.
P. O. Box 9104
290 Eliot Street
Ashland, MA 01721-9104

*Money Manager Verified
    Ratings*
P. O. Box 7634
Beverly Hills, CA 90212

Money Market Insight
IBC/Donoghue, Inc.
290 Eliot Street
P. O. Box 9104
Ashland, MA 01721-9104

*Moore Research Center
    Report*
Moore Research Center,
    Inc.
85180 Lorane Highway
Eugene, OR 97405

Morningstar Mutual Funds
Morningstar, Inc.
225 West Wacker Drive
Chicago, IL 60606-1228

Morry on the Market
50 Broadway, Suite 3700
New York, NY 10004

Municipal Bond Advisory
163 Amsterdam Avenue
Box 131
New York, NY 10023

Mutual Fund Letter
680 North Lakeshore
    Drive, Suite 2038
Chicago, IL 60611

Mutual Fund Monthly
525 B Street, Suite 1080
San Diego, CA 92101

No-Load Fund Investor
P. O. Box 318
Irvington-on-Hudson, NY
   10533-0318

No-Load Fund X
235 Montgomery Street,
   Suite 662
San Francisco, CA 94104-
   2994

100 Highest Yields
Bank Rate Monitor
P. O. Box 088888
North Palm Beach, FL
   33408-8888

*Perception for the
   Professional*
Butler Square Post Office
P. O. Box 300527
Minneapolis, MN 55403

Price Perceptions
Commodity Information
   Systems
210 Park Avenue,
   Suite 2970
Oklahoma City, OK
   73102-5604

*Proctor Investment
   Management*
217 Commerce Street
Greenville, NC 27858

*Professional Timing
   Service*
P. O. Box 7483
Missoula, MT 59807

Quantum
1272 West Pender Street
Vancouver, BC
CANADA V6E 2S8

*StraighTalk on Your
   Money*
7811 Montrose Road
Potomac, MD 20854

Systems and Forecasts
Signalert Corporation
150 Great Neck Road
Great Neck, NY 11021

Volume Reversal Survey
Almarco Trading
   Corporation
P. O. Box 1451
Sedona, AZ 86336

*World Investment Strategy
   Edge*
Pinnacle Capital
   Management, Inc.
4804 Laurel Canyon
   Boulevard, Suite 227
Valley Village, CA 91607

BOOKS

American Association of Individual Investors. *The Individual Investor's Low-Load Mutual Funds,* 13th ed. International Publishing Corp., 1994.

Bechter, Dan M. *The Federal Reserve Today,* 9th ed. Federal Reserve Bank of Richmond, 1992.

Berlin, Howard. *Handbook of Financial Market Indexes, Averages and Indicators.* Dow Jones-Irwin (now known as Irwin Professional Publishing), 1990.

Berlin, Howard. *Informed Investor's Guide to Financial Quotations.* Irwin Professional Publishing, 1994.

Cook, Timothy Q. and Robert K. LaRoche. *Instruments of the Money Market,* 7th ed. Federal Reserve Bank of Richmond, 1993.

Donoghue, William. *IBC/Donoghue's Mutual Funds Almanac,* 25th ed. IBC/Donoghue Organization, 1994.

Douglas, Livingston G. *Bond Risk Analysis: A Guide to Duration and Convexity.* New York Institute of Finance, 1990.

_____. *Yield Curve Analysis.* New York Institute of Finance, 1988.

Downes, John and Jordan Elliot Goodman. *Dictionary of Finance and Investment Terms,* 3rd ed. Barron's Educational Series, 1995.

Fabozzi, Frank J. *The Handbook of U.S. Treasury & Government Agency Securities: Instruments, Strategies, and Analysis.* Probus Publishing Co., 1990.

Fabozzi, Frank J. and T. Dessa Fabozzi. *The Handbook of Fixed Income Securities,* 4th ed. Irwin Professional Publishing, 1995.

Goodman, Jordan E. and Sonny Bloch. *Everyone's Money Book.* Dearborn Financial Publishing, 1994.

The Investment Company Institute's Directory of Mutual Funds. Investment Company Institute, 1994.

Jacobs, Sheldon. *The Handbook for No-Load Fund Investors,* 14th ed. No-Load Fund Investor, 1994.

Kroll, Stanley and Michael J. Paulenoff. *The Business One Irwin Guide to the Futures Markets.* Irwin Professional Publishing, 1993.

Shim, Joe K. and Joel K. Siegel. *Source: The Complete Guide to Investment Information...Where to Find It and How to Use It.* International Publishing Company, 1992.

Shook, R. J. and Robert L. Shook. *The Wall Street Dictionary.* New York Institute of Finance, 1990.

Taylor, Robert B. *Investor's Guide to Bonds,* KCI Communications, 1992.

Thau, Annette. *The Bond Book.* Probus Publishing Co., 1994.

Tucker, James F. *Buying Treasury Securities,* 16th ed. Federal Reserve Bank of Richmond, 1993.

Webb, Roy H. *Macroeconomic Data: A User's Guide,* 2nd ed. Federal Reserve Bank of Richmond, 1991.

PRIMARY DEALERS

The following primary dealers in government securities all publish market research and economic commentary. If you wish to be placed on a dealer's mailing list for updates, contact the office of the chief economist.

BA Securities, Inc.
    Bank Investment
    Securities Division
Bank of America Center
Box 37003
San Francisco, CA 94137

Barclays de Zoete Wedd
    Securities Incorporated
222 Broadway, 8th Floor
New York, NY 10038

Bear, Stearns & Co., Inc.
245 Park Avenue,
    4th Floor
New York, NY 10167

BT Securities Corporation
130 Liberty Street
New York, NY 10015

Chase Securities, Inc.
One Chase Plaza,
    35th Floor
New York, NY 10081

Chemical Securities, Inc.
270 Park Avenue,
    6th Floor
New York, NY 10017

Citicorp Securities Inc.
399 Park Avenue,
    7th Floor
New York, NY 10043

CS First Boston
55 East 52nd Street
Park Avenue Plaza
New York, NY 10055

Daiwa Securities America
    Inc.
One World Financial
    Center Tower A
200 Liberty St., 25th Floor
New York, NY 10043

Dean Witter Reynolds
    Inc.
Two World Trade Center
60th Floor
New York, NY 10048

Deutsche Bank Securities
    Corp.
31 West 52nd Street,
    4th Floor
New York, NY 10019

Dillon, Read & Co. Inc.
535 Madison Avenue
New York, NY 10022

Discount Corporation of
    New York, A Division
    of Zions First National
    Bank
58 Pine Street
New York, NY 10005

Donaldson, Lufkin &
    Jenrette Securities
    Corporation
140 Broadway
New York, NY 10005

Eastbridge Capital Inc.
135 East 57th Street
14th Floor
New York, NY 10022

First Chicago Capital
   Markets, Inc.
One First National Plaza
Suite 0463
Chicago, IL 60657-0463

Fuji Securities Inc.
Two World Trade Center
South Tower, 26th Floor
New York, NY 10281

Goldman Sachs & Co.
85 Broad Street,
   27th Floor
New York, NY 10004

Greenwich Capital
   Markets, Inc.
600 Steamboat Road
Greenwich, CT 06830

Harris-Nesbitt Thomson
   Securities Inc.
115 South La Salle Street
P.O. Box 1236
Chicago, IL 60690-1236

HSBC Securities, Inc.
40 Wall Street
New York, NY 10005

Kidder, Peabody & Co.
   Inc.
60 Broad Street, 5th Floor
New York, NY 10004

Aubrey G. Lanston & Co.,
   Inc.
One Chase Manhattan
   Plaza

53rd Floor
New York, NY 10005

Lehman Government
   Securities, Inc.
3 World Financial
   Center
New York, NY 10285-0900

Merrill Lynch Government
   Securities, Inc.
Merrill Lynch World
   Headquarters, North
   Tower
World Financial Center
New York, NY 10281

J.P. Morgan Securities
   Inc.
60 Wall Street
New York, NY 10260

Morgan Stanley & Co.
   Inc.
1221 Avenue of the
   Americas
New York, NY 10020

Nationsbanc Capital
   Markets, Inc.
7 Hanover Square
New York, NY 10004

The Nikko Securities Co.
   International, Inc.
One World Financial
   Center
Tower A
200 Liberty Street
New York, NY 10281

Nomura Securities International, Inc.
Two World Financial Center
Building B, 21st Floor
New York, NY 10281-1198

Paine Webber Incorporated
1285 Avenue of the Americas
11th Floor
New York, NY 10019

Prudential Securities Inc.
One Seaport Plaza, 27th Floor
New York, NY 10292

Salomon Brothers Inc.
Seven World Trade Center
42nd Floor
New York, NY 10048

Sanwa Securities (USA) Co., L.P.
599 Lexington Avenue
19th Floor
New York, NY 10022

SBC Government Securities Inc.
222 Broadway, Box 395
Church Street Station
New York, NY 10008

Smith Barney Shearson Inc.
1345 Avenue of the Americas
44th Floor
New York, NY 10105

UBS Securities Inc. (Subsidiary of Union Bank of Switzerland)
299 Park Avenue, 32nd Floor
New York, New York 10171

S.G. Warburg & Co., Inc.
787 Seventh Avenue, 26th Floor
New York, NY 10019

Yamaichi International (America), Inc.
Two World Trade Center
New York, NY 10048

INDEX

Accreted interest, 134
Accrued interest, 134
Agency securities, 129–130
Alternative Minimum Tax, 76, 122
Annualized rate of return, 17
    See also Yield
Approximate yield to maturity
    calculation, 47
Arbitrage, 134
Ask, 134
Auctions:
    treasury bills, 14
    treasury bonds, 26, 30
    treasury notes, 20, 23
Average weighted maturity, 98

Back up, 134
Bank reserves, 5–7
Barron's, 123
Basis point, 27, 134
Bearer bond, 25, 134
Benchmark bond, 29
Bid, 16, 135
Bond Brokers, 42–44
Bond funds, 97–105, 129,
    131–132
    average weighted maturity, 98
    closed ended, 119–120
    dividend reinvestment, 104–105
    expense ratio, 98
    loads, 102–104
    net asset value history, 98
    objectives, 98
    open ended, 129
    portfolios, 97–98
    selection, 102–105, 113–115,
        131–132
    total return, 98
    See also Mutual funds

Bond indenture, 135
Bond Market Semiotics, 64
Book-entry system, 25–26, 132,
    135
Bridgewater Daily Observations,
    66
Broker, 16, 42–44, 135
    selecting, 43–44
Business Week, 123

Call, 65–66, 115, 135
Callable, 135
Capital gain, 136
Carry, 135
Certificates of Deposit 12–13, 17
Chicago Board of Trade, 63
Chicago International Money
    market, 63
Closed-end funds, 119–120, 129
College funding, 34–35, 90–92,
    127–128
Commissions, 35–36, 81–82, 133,
    135
*Commodity Traders Consumer
    Report,* 67
Commodities. *See* Futures
Competitive bids, 135
Conservative investing, 11–13
Coupon, 32, 135
    See also Zero coupons
Coupon equivalent, 17
Credit risk, 38, 129–130, 135
    See also Safety
Current yield, 135
    calculation, 47

Dealer, 136
Debt, total public, 9
Derivative, 136

Discount bond, 23, 136
Discount rate calculation, 48
Dutch auction, 136

Early Economic Outlook, 52
Education bonds, 35, 90–92, 127–128
EE savings bonds, 35, 87–90
Encyclopedia of Closed-End Funds, 119
Exercise price, 136
Expiration date, 136

Federal Deposit Insurance Corporation (FDIC), 5, 53
Federal Farm Credit Banks (FFCB), 54–56
Federal funds, 136
  rate, 6–7, 136
Federal Home Loan Bank (FHLB), 54–56
Federal Home Loan Mortgage Corporation (Freddie Mac), 56
Federal National Mortgage Association (FNMA, Fannie Mae), 54, 56, 129–130
Federal Open Market Committee (FOMC), 2–4
Federal Reserve Board (FRB), 1–4, 136
  board of governors, 1–2
Federal Reserve System, 136
  branches, 141–144
  requirements, 136
Financial Assistance Corporation (FACO), 53, 56
Financial derivatives, 106–109
Financial pages, 45–48, 132–133
Financial planner, 136–137
Forbes, 123
Foreign investors, 68–70
  See also Global Markets
Forex market, 137
Form 1099-OID, 137
Full faith and credit guarantee, 53
FullerMoney, 69
Futures market, 57–64, 137
  limiting risks, 61–64

Global markets, 68–73
Government agency bonds, 53–56, 129–130
Government National Mortgage Association (Ginnie Mae), 56
Government obligation bonds, 83
Grant's Interest Rate Observer, 52
Griggs & Santow Report, 50
Guide to Low-Load Mutual Funds, 123

Handbook for No-Load Fund Investors, The, 80
Handle, 137
Humphrey-Hawkins Full-Growth Employment Investment Act, 1

Income investing, 22–24
Income taxes, 33, 74–77
Individual Retirement Accounts (IRA), 28, 33
Inflation, 2, 23, 137
Information sources:
  books, 154–155
  newsletters, 149–153
  newspaper financial pages, 45–47, 132–133
  radio, 147–149
  television, 144–147
Institutional Strategist, The, 72
Inter-American Development Bank, 56
Interest:
  accreted, 134
  accrued, 134
  rates, 1, 27, 29–30, 39
Interest-only "IO," 137
Inverse floater, 137
Investment Biker: On the Road with Jim Rogers, 71
Investment strategies, 124–126
Investor's Business Daily, 38

Keogh plans, 28, 33
Kiplinger's Personal Finance, 123

Leverage, 29, 57, 130–131, 137
Liabilities, matching, 34–35
Liquidity, 12, 137
Liscio Report, The, 73
Load, 133, 137
  See also Commission
London International Futures
  Exchange, 63
Long bond, 137
Long strip, 36
*Lynch Municipal Bond
  Advisory,* 81, 121

Margin, 137–138
Market:
  developing a consensus view,
    49–52
  international view, 68–70
Market value, 138
Matched sale, 7
*MBH Weekly Commodity
  Letter,* 49–50
Monetary policy, 1–4, 6
Money Magazine, 123
*Money Manager Verified
  Ratings,* 60
Money supply, 2–3
Moody's, 83
Morningstar Mutual Funds,
  107–108, 110–112, 115, 123
Morry on the Market, 63
Mortgage-backed security, 138
Municipal bonds, 75, 78–86, 138
  mutual funds, disadvantages
    of, 121–123
  zero coupons, 84
Mutual Fund News Service, 105,
  109
Mutual Fund Letter, The, 114
Mutual funds, 30–31, 93–96
  call options, 115
  closed-end, 119–120
  expense ratio, 98
  expenses, 110–112, 116–118
  fees, 98
  financial derivatives, 106–109
  municipal bonds, 121–123
  net asset value, 94
  objective, 98
  portfolio, 98

prospectuses, 98, 111–112
total return, 98
See also Bond funds

National Association of
  Securities Dealers, 81
Net asset value, 138
No-Load Fund Investor, The,
  121
NoLoad Fund X, 94, 103
Noncompetitive bid, 26,
  138
Noncallable, 138

Odd lot, 138
Off-the-run issue, 138
On-the-run issue, 138
Open Market Desk, 3
Open-end funds, 129

Pension plans, 127
Phantom income, 33
Portfolio, laddered, 85
Premium bond, 22–23, 138
Price Perceptions, 61
Primary dealers, 8–10, 138,
  155–158
Principal-only "PO," 138
Put, 66, 138

Quantum, 73

Repurchase agreement (RP,
  Repo), 7, 138–139
Residential Funding
  Corporation (Refco), 56
Reverse repurchase agreement,
  7, 139
Risk, 129–130
  See also Safety
Round lot, 139

Safety, 25–27, 129–130
Savings Bond Question &
  Answer Book, The, 89
Savings bonds, 87–92, 127–128,
  139
  college funding, 90–92,
    127–128
Secondary market, 27, 139

Separate Trading of Registered Interest and Principal of Securities (STRIPS), 32–33
Series EE Savings Bonds, 35, 87–90
Series HH Savings Bonds, 88–89
Settlement date, 139
Short sale, 139
Short strip, 36
Singapore International Monetary Exchange, 63
Smart Money, 123
Spread, 139
Standard & Poor's, 83
Stripped Treasuries *See* Zero Coupons
Structured notes, 106–107, 139
Student Loan Marketing Corporation (Sallie Mae), 55–56, 129–130
Sydney Futures Exchange, 63

Tax Reform Act of 1986, 34
Taxes, 33, 74–77
  exemptions, 55
Tender, 15, 26
Tennessee Valley Authority, 55
Trade date, 140
Trade deficit, 51
Treasury auctions, 8
Treasury bills, 11–13, 48, 140
  auctions, 14
  benefits of, 11–12
  book entry form, 25–26, 132, 135
  compared to cash, 11
  compared to CD's, 12–13
  discount, 48
  maturities, 14
  minimum purchase, 14
  monitoring prices of, 16
  purchasing, 14–18, 128–129
  registered form of issuance, 26
  safety, 25–27
  selling, 16
  yield to maturity, 48
Treasury bonds, 25–27, 140
  auctions, 26, 30
  benchmark bond, 29
  book entry form, 25–26

futures, 28
maturity, 25–26
mutual funds, 30
purchasing, 26
tender, 26
volatility, 28–31
Treasury Direct, 15, 20, 140
Treasury futures, 57–64
  limiting risk, 61–64
  options, 65–67
Treasury Investors Growth Receipt (TIGRs), 33
Treasury Notes, 19–21, 22–24, 140
  auctions, 20, 23
  compared to treasury bills, 19–20
  customers for, 20
  investment strategies, 20–24
  maturity, 19–20, 22
  mutual funds, 30
  premium, 22–23
  purchasing, 20
  uncallable, 21

Volatility, 28–31, 140

Wall Street Journal, 38, 39, 47, 86, 103
Wasting asset, 67
World Bank, 56
Worth, 123

Yield:
  curve, 37–41, 140
  floor, 12
  to maturity, 47–48, 140

Zero-coupon bonds, 28, 32–36, 127, 140
  commissions, 35–36
  investment strategies, 36
  maturities, 32
  municipals, 84
  long strip, 36
  phantom income, 33
  shopping for, 34–36
  short strip, 36
  treasuries, 32–36, 127
  volatility, 35

NOTES

NOTES